SELLING OUTSIDE
YOUR CULTURE ZONE

A Guide for Sales Success in Today's
Cross-Cultural Marketplace

Earl D. Honeycutt, Ph.D.
Elon University

Lew Kurtzman
Growth Resources Associates

BEHAVIORAL SCIENCES RESEARCH PRESS, INC.
Dallas, Texas

Behavioral Sciences Research Press, Inc.

12803 Demetra Drive

Dallas, Texas 75234

Dell is a registered trademark of Dell Inc.

Donald Trump is a registered trademark of Trump, Donald J.

General Motors is a registered trademark of General Motors Corporation.

Martha Stewart is a registered trademark of Martha Stewart Living Omnimedia, Inc.

Mercedes is a registered trademark of DaimlerChrysler.

Outback Steakhouse is a registered trademark of Outback Steakhouse of Florida, Inc.

Rolex is a registered trademark of Rolex Watch U.S.A., Inc.

Wal-Mart is a registered trademark of Wal-Mart Stores, Inc.

The characters, companies, and events in the buyer-seller exchange scenarios in this book are fictitious. Any similarity to real companies or persons, living or dead, is coincidental and not intended by the authors.

Library of Congress Catalog Number: 2006921824

ISBN-10: 0-935907-11-4 (PBK)

ISBN-13: 978-0-935907-11-7 (PBK)

1 2 3 4 5 6 7 8 9 10

Printed in the United States of America

Cover and interior design by Lightbourne, Inc.

EDH: To Laura, Travis, Andrea, and Cole

LK: To Margie

ACKNOWLEDGMENTS

Writing a book is seldom, if ever, the sole work of the authors. Therefore, we acknowledge the insightful comments and suggestions of Jeff Tanner (Baylor University), Robert Ingram (GlaxoSmithKline), Chuck Smith (Payment Processing, Inc.), George Dudley and Shannon Goodson (Behavioral Sciences Research Press, Inc.), Kevin Yoder (Astra Zeneca), Shawn Thelen (Hofstra University), Coleman Rich (Elon University), Robert Keating (UNC-Wilmington), Ann Alexander (Greensboro *News & Record*), and Angela Pimentel (GlaxoSmithKline). Also, without the support and encouragement of Dean John Burbridge, Associate Dean Scott Buechler, and Departmental Chairs Matt Valle and Betsy Stevens at the Love School of Business at Elon University, this project would not have been possible.

It is also important to acknowledge educators who motivated us to learn about and explore different cultures and beliefs. Our sincere thanks and respect are extended to Dr. Marvin Williamsen (Appalachian State University), Dr. Jack Merchant (CSU-Sacramento), Dr. B.J. Dunlap (Western Carolina University), Dr. John Ford (Old Dominion University), and Dr. Hiram C. Barksdale (University of Georgia).

CONTENTS

PREFACE

At the dawn of the 21st century, it is apparent that U.S. population growth is being fueled by racial and ethnic minorities. For example, Hispanics accounted for almost half the population growth (40.6%) between 2000 and 2004 and now total 41.3 million persons living in the U.S.[1] In California alone, more than 10 percent of the population is Asian.[2] The Asian population matched the Hispanic growth of 17 percent during this same time period, while the African-American population increased by more than five percent. Demographers were surprised to learn that Hispanic growth is driven by two factors: immigration and, perhaps more importantly, homegrown births.[3] Given these trends, it is important for sales managers and salespersons to understand that

- More than 110 languages are spoken in the U.S. today.[4]

- By 2050, non-Anglo Americans will comprise only half of the U.S. population.[5]

- Approximately 185 million persons world-wide live outside their country of birth.[6]

These important facts demonstrate how diverse the U.S. as a nation is growing, and these changes mean that buyer-seller interactions are becoming more complex when

- Communicating across language and accent barriers.
- Developing and maintaining business relationships despite different values.

While it appears intuitive that salespersons and sales managers will interact more and more with customers/buyers who were born and raised in other cultures, writing about cultural differences is not easy. Explaining culture in a clear and purposeful way can be tricky in that it is easy to offend someone when making a generalization, faulty statement, or an error of fact. If *we* make any of these mistakes, we urge you to keep in mind that every effort has been made to be as accurate as possible. We also offer a sincere apology for any inconsistencies—we assure you that we have no desire to offend any of our readers, whether they are mainline U.S. or new citizens.

This book begins with an introductory chapter that defines "culture zone" and explains how culture impacts sales situations. Chapter 2 then poses questions that allow you to determine the "width" of your culture zone. In Chapter 3, the links between culture, cross-cultural communication, and personal selling are explained. Chapter 4 introduces a sales process that is designed for cross-cultural settings. Chapter 5 is a gathering of eleven actual cross-cultural scenarios that end in disaster. The authors analyze each scenario and discuss what went wrong and how the salesperson could have safely navigated the encounter. Chapter 6, the final chapter, consolidates the lessons put forward in the book and offers a framework for success when *Selling Outside Your Culture Zone*.

We compiled this book from personal experiences, and a number of written sources are provided in the reference section of this book. The reference section lists the books and periodicals that appear in the footnotes of each chapter. Appendix 4 offers the reader additional cross-cultural resources that, when appropriate, may be consulted or purchased to expand the reader's knowledge and understanding of culture in general and specific cultural practices.

Earl D. Honeycutt, Ph.D., Elon University

Lew Kurtzman, Growth Resources Associates

1

WHAT IS A CULTURE ZONE?

Culture influences everything humans do, including the way they think, feel, and act.[1] Salespersons need to understand that "culture is the way in which a group solves problems and reconciles dilemmas."[2] Given the impact of culture on all that we do, have you ever wondered how many sales have been lost because you did not understand your buyer's culture?** Like most sales representatives, you are probably unsure of the correct answer. So, imagine that you are the salesperson or the sales manager of the sales rep involved in the following buyer-seller interchange.

> **Salesperson:** *So, Mr. Sakai, I'm sure you agree that the Model 620 has all the bells and whistles that you could ask for.*
>
> **Sakai:** **(smiling, long pause)** *Bell and whistle???*
>
> **Salesperson:** *You know—it's the Cadillac of the industry.*
>
> **Sakai:** *Like automobile???*
>
> **Salesperson:** *You know what I mean.*
>
> **Sakai:** *Ah, you mean Model 620 expensive like Cadillac.*

** Go to Appendix 1 and determine your *current* Culture Zone Quotient (CZQ).

Salesperson: *No. I mean it's the best.*

Sakai: *Best bell and whistle???*

Salesperson: *Yes. It has all the best bells and whistles.*

Sakai: *Why it need bell and whistle???*

Salesperson: *It doesn't really have bells and whistles.*

Sakai: *So why you say it have bell and whistle???*

Salesperson: *You know, it's state-of-the-art.*

Sakai: *Ah, stateoftheart (???????)*

Salesperson: *Yes. In fact it even has a static sound suppression system.*

Sakai: *Why it have that?*

Salesperson: *It suppresses the sound of the static ringing.*

Sakai: *But you say it have no bell. No whistle either.*

Salesperson: *That's not what I meant. I'm not sure you understand what I'm trying to say. I apologize. I wish I spoke Chinese.*

Sakai: *I not speak Chinese either. Just English and Japanese!!!*

Because of important demographic shifts taking place in the North American and European marketplaces, salespersons cannot rely upon sales techniques learned and practiced in the past. In this scenario, the salesperson employs metaphors to describe the quality of a new product. The metaphoric approach, however, only further confuses Mr. Sakai! To succeed with customers in today's diverse marketplace, a salesperson must increasingly understand how to successfully interact with decision-makers that were born and educated in unfamiliar countries, cultures, languages, and customs. Also, growing numbers of purchasing agents, engineers, and managers represent disparate cultures, genders, and ethnicities. Therefore, it is imperative for today's sales professionals to approach potential customers with cultural insight, sensitivity, and confidence that exist outside their own culture zone.

This book highlights common unintentional situations that are encountered when selling to buyers from outside your culture zone. *Culture zone* is defined as an array of skills and abilities, starting with empathy and understanding, that one uses to successfully interact in sales situations with individuals from other cultures. Thus, a salesperson that possesses a wide culture zone utilizes a high degree of ability to adapt and work constructively with a diverse buyer base. Conversely, a salesperson with a narrow culture zone demonstrates a limited ability to reach successful outcomes with buyers from different cultural backgrounds.

What a salesperson must never do is stereotype. When people stereotype individuals from other cultures, they point out what is different rather than what is familiar (see Exhibit 1-1). Such behavior is dangerous, when either positive or negative stereotypes are employed, for a variety of reasons that are explained below and shown in Exhibit 1-2. First, a stereotype is a narrow view of behavior that is exaggerated by the observer. Second, the observer often equates anything different as being wrong. Third, a person who stereotypes forgets that within a culture, people behave within a range of behaviors based upon their personality. So, a *stereotype* is a generalization applied to all members of a cultural, racial, or religious group regardless of their individual differences.

A stereotype is quite different from the guidelines provided in this book. For example, saying that Asian buyers tend to be more group- or family-oriented than U.S. buyers is meant to be a starting point for understanding this group of buyers. We

EXHIBIT 1-1

Common Negative and Positive Stereotypes

Group	Negative Stereotypes	Positive Stereotypes
Italian	Mafia affiliation, greasy, untrustworthy	Family-oriented, loyal, romantic
Jewish	Cheap, greedy, brash	Smart, talented, compassionate
Irish	Drinker, womanizer, hell-raiser	Charitable, fun loving, charming
French	Arrogant, sarcastic, cowardly	Connoisseur, sophisticated, artistic
Hispanic/ Latino	Compulsive, uneducated, lazy	Warm, friendly, loyal
British	Formal, stiff, regimented	Classy, proper, courteous

categorically state that all Asian buyers do not behave one way in sales situations and that the salesperson should use the information provided in this book to initiate sales meetings with an individual. The difference is that stereotypical statements are inflexible—the assumption is that everyone in the group behaves in a certain way and there is no room for individual differences. The general facts presented in this book are merely guidelines, or starting points, to assist salespersons who call upon buyers who originally lived in another culture. When we say, for example, that a Filipino-American is likely to say "yes" to keep from hurting your feelings when something else is actually meant, we remind the reader that this guidance does not apply to all Filipino-American buyers that one encounters.

EXHIBIT 1-2
The Dangers of Stereotyping

As early as 1725, John Lienhard defined stereotype as "cast[ing] a person in a preset mold—to deny individuality." Even today, *Webster's New World Dictionary* defines stereotype as "a fixed or conventional notion [about] a person, group, or idea...." To help us better understand someone from another culture who is unfamiliar to us, we may make assumptions or generalizations about that group of people to make them familiar to us. Generalizing this way can help us learn about others, but stereotyping becomes dangerous if unrealistic and inaccurate characteristics are ascribed to a group from another culture. To become culturally aware, you must first understand yourself. Then you can begin to understand others.

Adapted from: "The Dangers of Stereotyping," by Joyce Millet, www.cultural-savvy.com, December 3, 2004.

WHY PEOPLE STEREOTYPE

Most people stereotype to relieve anxiety over ambiguous situations or unknown behavior. By stereotyping, humans reduce uncertainty by placing groups of people into tidy categories, or boxes, which predict behavior.[3] For these reasons, citizens from most cultures stereotype. However, stereotyping fits exceptionally well within the existing European-American culture in the U.S. For example, most European-Americans are linear thinkers, rational, and tend to look for cause and effect relationships. When faced with uncertainty, it is easier to stereotype in order to explain disparate behavior than to admit that something is not understood. A serious problem arises when we interact with

someone from another culture and they conform to our stereotype. We then assume we were right all along and attribute
greater weight to the stereotypical behavior than is warranted.
Said differently, we reinforce our stereotype about a group based
upon one or more actions displayed by a single individual.

WHY STEREOTYPES ARE INCORRECT

Members of cultural, racial, or religious groups tend to vary
individually in a number of ways. Perhaps the most important is socio-economic status. This means that the behavior
and attitudes of members of cultural groups differ based upon
their educational level, social standing, and financial status. For
example, immigrants from Taiwan who hold graduate degrees,
come from professional families, and bring funds with them to
start a business, will certainly view things differently during a
sales call than will an immigrant who escaped Vietnam by boat
in 1975 and then worked hard upon arriving in the U.S. to save
enough money to start their own business.

Second, individuals from different regions of a country can
vary as much in their behavior and attitudes as can people in
the U.S. who live in California and Alabama. The same is true of
buyers from London and the countryside of England.

Age can also result in differences. For example, older citizens from India may adhere to traditional beliefs more so than
younger Indian buyers who grew up and attended college in the
U.S. Likewise, gender is important. Men from Mexico and the
Middle East tend to be more assertive and direct than women
from these nations.

The length of time one has lived in the U.S. may be the most
difficult influence to predict. Some immigrants embrace U.S.
culture while others speak their native language at night, travel

"home" every holiday and vacation, and remain dedicated to their culture. As implied above, if a Cuban, Vietnamese, or East German came to the U.S. for survival, their behavior and attitudes will probably differ markedly from a citizen of Mexico who immigrated to the U.S. to pursue the American economic dream.

Lastly, and with no desire to further confuse the reader, an individual can also behave differently under unlike circumstances. That is, in times of pressure or chaos, underlying cultural attitudes and coping mechanisms can emerge and affect buyer behavior. This means that culture can affect behavior years after the person immigrates and begins assimilating their present culture.

WHY STEREOTYPES ARE DANGEROUS

The use of stereotypes is dangerous because it prevents us from seeing people for the individuals they are. To believe that all African-Americans are good athletes or that all Asians are inscrutable causes us not to value the traits each individual possesses. Perhaps most importantly, stereotypes can be self-fulfilling. For example, if a salesperson stereotypes that the buyer from France is arrogant toward Americans, then the salesperson may be overly sensitive to words or actions that can be perceived to be arrogant. This results in reduced communication and relationships, plus a higher probability that trust and a relationship will not occur.

HOW CAN STEREOTYPES BE MINIMIZED?

First, you need to become aware of the stereotypes you have formed. One way to identify stereotypes is to form a list of cultural groups in the U.S. as shown in Exercise 1-1 below.

EXERCISE 1-1
Becoming Aware of Stereotypes

Group	Beliefs about Group	Source(s)
Chinese		
Japanese		
Filipinos		
African-Americans		
Russians		
European-Americans		

Now, jot down your beliefs about each group and the source(s) of your information. For example, let's suppose you believe all Japanese are smart business people and that you remember hearing about Japanese business success in the TV news media. What about the other groups listed above? Can you list your beliefs about each one and the origin of the information? If the results of your writing appear that you hold stereotypes about each group, do not despair. This is fairly typical. Another problem for most people completing this exercise is that they are less able to complete the European-American category. Since the majority of U.S. citizens are currently of European derivation, fewer stereotypes are held about one's own cultural group.

When you have experiences with other cultural groups, however, it is more difficult to lump people into a single group.

The purpose of this book is to help current and future salespersons broaden their culture zone, *without stereotyping*, in order to achieve successful sales results with a diverse population of buyers. We accomplish this goal by providing the reader with an increased understanding of culture and guidance for cross-cultural interactions so that common mistakes are minimized when selling in unfamiliar cultural situations.

This is what *Selling Outside Your Culture Zone* is all about. Over the years, many salespeople have become comfortable selling to buyers from their own cultural, gender, religious, and age groups. Most traditional sales training emphasizes selling skills that are oriented toward Western society and ignore the nuance of culture, even though the backgrounds of buyers in U.S. and European markets are shifting dramatically. For example, the U.S. Census Bureau reports that 12 percent of the 2000 U.S. population, or more than thirty million people, were born outside the U.S. This demographic fact implies that a cultural gap is growing between sellers and buyers who were born, matured, and educated in distant lands with different business rituals and social expectations. This cultural diversity trend is predicted to continue expanding well into the mid-21st century. As seen in the figure below, the fastest growing immigrant group is the Latino/Spanish-American segment.

Actual stories and dialogues that illustrate the confusion and frustration that can occur when the seller is insensitive or unaware of cultural differences, that create barriers to successful interactions, are discussed throughout the book. Accents, facial expressions, and voice tone can be obstacles to *trust*, an absolutely essential component of the buyer-seller relationship. Without trust, no matter the culture, little or no business will occur. Distinct cultures require different behavior to establish

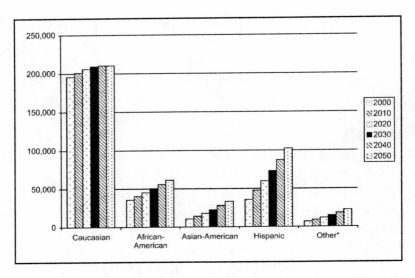

Projected U.S. Population Growth by Race (2000–2050). *Includes American Indian and Alaska Native alone, Native Hawaiian and Other Pacific Islander alone, and two more races. Adapted from the U.S. Census Bureau, international database.

trust. For a salesperson, developing a wider culture zone requires three actions: *recognition, respect,* and *reconciliation.*[4]

Recognition:

- understanding your own cultural makeup
- familiarity with the cultural environment entered

Respect:

- empathy and respect for the buyer's culture
- never stereotyping

Reconciliation:

- approaching the customer with cultural insight
- possessing a strong desire to communicate
- remaining flexible and patient during sales encounters

As a result of learning more about different culture zones, especially one's own, today's sales professional will be more comfortable and successful when entering cross-cultural selling situations where both buyer and seller struggle to understand, communicate, and trust one another in their search for a "win-win agreement." Thus, another goal of this book is to help both buyers and sellers conduct a more effective sales process that includes fewer misunderstandings, less frustration, and ultimately, a smoother, more acceptable, and longer-lasting business relationship.

CHAPTER 1 TAKE-AWAY POINTS:

- Culture influences everything humans do.
- Culture determines how buyers and sellers solve problems and reconcile dilemmas.
- A salesperson's successfully employed skills and abilities make up their cultural comfort zone.
- Stereotyping occurs when we generalize and point out differences between ourselves and other persons.
- Within each cultural group, individuals differ based upon age, education, personality, and socio-economic status.
- Stereotyping is dangerous when it becomes a self-fulfilling prophecy.
- The cultural makeup of the U.S. marketplace is changing significantly.
- To develop a wider cultural comfort zone, a salesperson must: Recognize, Respect, and Reconcile the buyer's culture.

2

HOW WIDE IS YOUR
CULTURE ZONE?

We have all, no doubt, experienced the awkward situation of trying to communicate and interact with a person that was born and raised in a different country or culture. Even though our new friend dresses and speaks like we do, they also possess less apparent cultural traits, customs, attitudes, and mannerisms. Language and accents are easily identified, as is cultural clothing worn on a daily basis. But when cultural misunderstandings go unrecognized and hamper sales interactions, both buyer and seller can become frustrated and business will be lost.

Selling to buyers from different cultures is extremely important now that minority groups comprise 25 percent of U.S. households and account for 20 percent of annual consumer spending, or $460 billion.[1] Also, a growing number of engineers, managers, and technical professionals in business-to-business (B2B) situations have recently relocated to the U.S. Even second-generation buyers unconsciously adhere to cultural beliefs passed on by their parents, and these innate perceptions can influence their purchase decisions. Both the consumer and business marketplaces offer great opportunity for contemporary sales professionals, but prospective customers must be approached and sold to within *their* culture zone.

The purpose of this chapter is to explain how culture impacts both buyers and sellers in sales situations.

New arrivals to the U.S. bring hidden cultural influences to their adopted home. For example, in some cases, religious and political beliefs may be stronger than interpersonal relations or product capabilities in determining a buying decision. Personal bias and prejudice about certain groups can work either in favor of or against the salesperson. Nonetheless, as long as there is a need, funding, and the authority to purchase, the cross-cultural buyer is a highly valued potential customer; but firms seldom base their sales quotas and goals upon a salesperson's ability to work successfully with customers from different ethnic backgrounds and cultural origins. The following salesperson was insensitive to cultural differences and, unquestionably, approached the customer from a narrow culture zone.

INAPPROPRIATE USE OF HUMOR

In this scenario, Fred Johnson is calling upon Mr. Singh, who recently arrived from India, about a new computer for his small business.

> **Johnson:** *Looks like you're leaning toward the model G 24, Mr. Singh. Good choice.*
>
> **Singh:** *Vell, I'm still on de-fence.*
>
> **Johnson:** *I guess that puts me on of-fence.*
>
> **Singh:** *What?*
>
> **Johnson:** *You said that you were on de-fence. I'm only kidding.*
>
> **Singh:** *What is de joke?*

Johnson: *De-fence. Of-fence. Get it?*

Singh: *I don't know what is so funny. Good day!*

This is an excellent example of *careless remarks* in the form of inappropriate humor that turned into unintentional ridicule. The salesman, Fred Johnson, made a quick rejoinder to a common phrase. However, Mr. Singh concluded that the salesperson was making fun of his accent. It was the salesman's conditioned response to anyone who said they were "sitting on the fence." One must wonder if the salesperson thought Mr. Singh would think the careless remark was humorous. In reflection, it is apparent that the salesperson spoke without thinking.

When meeting with customers, no matter their origins, salespersons must be careful about what they say. As discussed in the section on culture, salespersons must think before speaking to minimize careless remarks, the use of idioms, and double-meaning words. Johnson was certainly not trying to be malicious in his response to Mr. Singh. However, his unintentional remark offended Mr. Singh, and it will take much time and effort to mend the relationship—*if* Mr. Singh will accept Johnson's apology and trust him again. It is difficult to repair a broken relationship no matter how trivial the cause. Fred Johnson would have fared better by asking Mr. Singh: "May I ask why you are on the fence?" Or perhaps, "It is natural to be uncertain about such an important decision. What information can I provide to help you?" Either question potentially elicits information about why Mr. Singh was still undecided about the salesperson's product.

Humor is serious business in sales. It can be very effective or it can kill the sale. Before making clever jokes, or repeating a "good one" that was received by E-mail, it is imperative to understand the buyer's cultural background. Such a determination should be made, if possible, prior to the initial contact.

Even a cursory phone call can reveal clues about the buyer that allows the salesperson to correctly plan the best approach at the initial sales meeting. If the salesperson is meeting the buyer for the first time, the employment of humor should be approached cautiously, if at all.

GETTING IT RIGHT. APPROPRIATE USE OF HUMOR

Now, let's consider a sales call made by senior sales rep Sandy Duffy of Jaffe Container Company, a manufacturer of cardboard boxes. Sandy is visiting with Mario Colevito, owner of the Italian Gardens Pizza Emporium, within his culture zone.

> **Sandy:** *Mario, good to see you. How is Donna? Joey and Angie?*
>
> **Mario:** *Great, Sandy. The family is good. How about yours?*
>
> **Sandy:** *Carol and the kids are fine. Larry is graduating next month.*
>
> **Mario:** *My Angie, she just get engaged.*
>
> **Sandy:** *Nice Italian boy?*
>
> **Mario:** *More like antipasto. Y'know, a bit 'a this, a little 'a that. A nica boy though.*
>
> **Sandy:** *I'm sure. He'll be Italian once you start feeding him. When is the wedding?*
>
> **Mario:** *No date yet. I'll let you know when.*
>
> **Sandy:** *Please do. I'd like to send them a nice gift.*
>
> **Mario:** *So, Sandy. What-a you try to sell me today?*
>
> **Sandy:** *We've got a new line of pizza boxes I'd like you to see.*

Mario: *What could be new in a pizza box? We buy the same ones for years. No bigga deal.*

Sandy: *How about when the top droops from the steam and it comes into contact with the cheese? Do your customers ever complain about that?*

Mario: *Yeh, once in a while, but a pizza box is a pizza box. I still got about three hundred that I buy from you last month.*

Sandy: *Don't worry, Mario. You're a good friend and customer. I'll take the old ones and replace them with new if you just give them a try.*

Mario: *What's the bigga deal with your new box? Some kinda' gimmick? I don't want no fancy gimmicks.*

Sandy: *No gimmick, just a stronger reinforced top. Keeps it from drooping into the cheese.*

Mario: *More money, right?*

Sandy: *Hey, Mario. You make the best pizza this side of Italy. Do you want it ruined by a lousy pizza box? When people open the box at home, they'll thank you for the new box and tell their friends and neighbors about it. You'll get a lot more deliveries.*

Mario: *Sandy, you're a hell of a salesman. I'll give 'em a try. Now, how about I maka you a nica pizza.*

Sandy: *The usual, Mario—pepperoni and onions.*

Several things in this scenario are obvious. First, Sandy and Mario appear to have a great relationship. Both men sincerely ask about the other's family. Second, we observe humor in the dialogue, but the salesperson understands his customer's humor and laughs with—not at—him. Finally, Sandy offers the product with a clear benefit that includes exchanging the items most recently sold to the customer. This scenario appears to be a win-win situation for everyone.

Most persons who are educated and raised outside the U.S. speak English with an accent. Even in English-speaking countries like India, the Philippines, Jamaica, Australia, and New Zealand, pronunciations, words, and verbal expressions differ markedly from those utilized in North America. While such differences may be fun to compare, they should only be raised when and if everyone understands and agrees that the humor is to be taken lightly and, by all means, impersonally. As seen in the first scenario that involved Mr. Singh, the most likely outcome for salespersons who use humor inappropriately is disaster, including hard feelings and lost sales.

To prepare for today's multicultural marketplace and to gauge the width of your culture zone, ask yourself the following questions:

CAN I ACCEPT THAT PEOPLE ARE DIFFERENT, WITHOUT JUDGING THEM?

In most English-speaking cultures, people tend to act based upon several beliefs or assumptions. First, social engagements, like sales calls, are driven by practical rather than emotional concerns. That is, when a salesperson visits a potential buyer, the stated purpose is to help the buyer operate more efficiently, save money, or purchase the latest technology while making a profit. But this is not true of all cultures. Buyers in many cultures allow feelings and emotions to enter into or even dominate the purchase equation. Second, U.S. citizens tend to perceive their society to be "classless." The phrase "All men (and women) are created equal..." is assumed to be true. Most Americans understand that this is an ideal rather than a reality in the U.S. In other cultures, however, one remains in the class into which they were born no matter their accomplishments. A person's family or class is known, and the respect and prestige they receive emanates from these facts. Conversely, in the U.S., citizens focus more on merit than group membership. Even when people do not belong to the correct country club, live in the right neighborhood, or graduate from a respected college or university, business success can trump initial social status in the U.S. In other cultures, however, this is not possible. In order to succeed in many cultures, it is absolutely essential for the businessperson to be born into the correct group. Thus, an important question you should ask yourself is: *can I accept that people from different cultures exhibit unique behavior, beliefs, and thought processes?*

WHAT ARE MY CULTURAL ORIENTATIONS?

Given that people from distinct cultures behave differently, you act the way you do when you interact with customers based upon your own cultural beliefs. When you meet a customer, try to solve a problem, or socialize, you will view your actions—and those of your customers—through the cultural lens you acquired from your family, community, and nation. Think about the potential misunderstandings that can occur when you and your customer grew up in different countries and cultures.

For example, how do you view the world? Are you action-oriented? If you see a problem, do you rush to fix it? How do you view your environment? Do you believe that people should control or live in harmony with their environment? When focusing on time, do you feel that it must be precisely observed? Do you get irritated if someone is late for an appointment? Is your communication style direct or indirect? How important is power in your interactions? Can you conform to group norms or must you act as an individual? These are not easy questions to answer.[2]

What might surprise you is that while most of the questions raised above appear to have two extremes, there are a range of positions that fall along a continuum. By this time, you should understand that people from distinct cultures are likely to view the world and their daily actions very differently. Such attitudes and behavior do not make you right and your buyers wrong, or vice-versa. They simply make us different in how we all think and act. Understanding cultural orientations is important because different sales strategies and methods must be employed when two or more people from diverse cultures interact.

HOW ADAPTABLE AM I?

Since buyers from different cultures think and act distinctly, your cultural perspectives will often be at odds with these individuals. Another important question is: can you adapt to successfully interact with your buyers? One can adopt another culture—we can move to a new locale and, through concerted effort, learn and accept new ways of thinking and acting. What is more difficult, however, is to adapt to different cultures. A salesperson may need to adapt to buyers from several different cultures each day. A culturally aware salesperson comes to understand how buyers think and what factors influence their decisions. This allows the salesperson to change their behavior to best match buyer needs. Said differently, the salesperson must understand the customer and then tailor an approach that best satisfies buyer needs. A salesperson that cannot or will not adapt to distinctive customers will have difficulty succeeding in today's culturally diverse sales environment.

WHAT DO I NEED TO
KNOW ABOUT CULTURES?

Most importantly, you must understand the role that culture plays in the sales process. Simply stated, *culture influences everything we do in life.* Thus, to correctly interpret sales situations, the salesperson must understand basic cultural influences. In specific situations, more detailed cultural knowledge is essential. For example, when *initially* calling upon a German engineer, one must understand that it is important to be formal in discussions, to not call the engineer by his first name unless given permission, and to stress logic and functionality in the sales approach. Germans tend to be reserved and have a reputation for being meticulous and methodical. It is not unusual for the buyer to schedule meetings that include technical persons in order to confirm details of the offer.[3] Simply understanding these general characteristics of buyers from Germany provides the salesperson with significant insight for planning their sales call. However, the German buyer may also be influenced by their individual personality and the amount of U.S. culture they have adopted since moving to the U.S. Thus, the salesperson would approach the German buyer in a formal manner, have a logical and detailed presentation, and understand that if the buyer is reserved, that is normal. But, once face-to-face, the salesperson may have to adapt their interactions if the buyer is less formal or makes special requests of the seller. There are numerous sources, listed in Appendix 4, that provide general recommendations for successfully interacting with potential and current customers who are from different cultures. Remember, the recommendations offered in this book are only starting points for the salesperson.

WHERE DO I GO FROM HERE?

The next chapter explores culture in detail. Culture can be organized into eight distinct sub-areas to help you understand the different ways people think and act. It is essential that you learn and understand the eight components of culture in order to apply them to your own interactions with customers. Now, let's take a closer look at culture.

CHAPTER 2 TAKE-AWAY POINTS:

- Buyers from other cultures now comprise 25 percent of U.S. households.

- A growing number of multinational engineers, managers, and technical B2B professionals work in the U.S.

- Humor is serious business in sales—it can be very effective or it can kill the sale.

- Can you accept that buyers from other countries think and act differently?

- Do you understand your own cultural orientation?

- Can you adapt to distinct cultural situations?

- Do you understand the role culture plays in the sales process?

3

LINKING CULTURE AND SALES

Culture influences everything we do as humans, especially our thoughts and actions. *Culture* is defined as *all human behavior that we acquire from and share with members of our society.* Culture is not inherited. It is learned from the family and society in which we are born and raised. Potential problems arise in sales situations when cultural components like communication practices, religious beliefs, education levels, views of beauty, social organizations, attitudes toward technology, time perspectives, and values/norms cause misunderstandings between buyers and sellers. When there are cultural misunderstandings, there is an increased likelihood of sales being lost.

When salespersons and managers are sensitive to different cultural practices, the chance of success in interpersonal relationships improves. When a salesperson approaches a sales meeting with a potential customer from a different culture, with a general understanding of that person's cultural beliefs, the salesperson's words, actions, and body language can be tailored to increase the potential of successfully interacting with that individual. Understanding culture allows salespersons to minimize conflict and maximize the effectiveness of relationship building through correct thoughts, feelings, and behaviors.

When a salesperson comes into contact with a buyer from a different culture, additional knowledge will be learned from each encounter. One becomes *assimilated* after completely absorbing a new culture—which is rare. However, the level of *acculturation* can vary based upon the amount of culture learned and accepted by a person. An important point to remember is that the greater the degree of cultural accord that exists between the salesperson and the potential buyer, the higher the probability of business success. That is why it is imperative for salespeople to understand and feel comfortable working among the different levels of culture.

DIFFERENT CULTURAL LEVELS

Human behavior is influenced by cultural levels that include global, national, local, and company cultures.

Global cultures appear to be blending as consumers worldwide are exposed to movies, cable/satellite television, and magazines that advertise global brand products. This creates consumers that possess similar needs, wants, and knowledge about the goods they purchase. However, when approaching potential buyers from a distinct culture, it is naive to assume they buy in exactly the same way and for the same reasons. Even though consumers are familiar with and desire such global brands as Mercedes®, Rolex®, and Dell®, they will most likely purchase these products based upon distinct decision influences and the purchase process they have learned in their home culture.

National culture is the most important cultural level for salespersons to understand because it has the greatest impact on consumer and buyer behavior. National culture is composed of five distinct dimensions.

1. **Power distance.** Indicates the extent to which members of a culture accept unequal distribution of power. Some

cultures accept larger power distances between members of society or the organization, which impacts the buyer-seller relationship. In other words, some societies view the parties involved in each social interaction as being equal or unequal. The level of power distance defines the roles played by members of that society, especially salespersons. When dealing with owners, managers, or scientists from cultures with large power distances, it is imperative to not act too familiar and to use formal titles, unless instructed to address them informally. One of the authors has known Japanese managers for more than a decade and neither party addresses the other by their first names. For the American, it is always "Saito san" or Mr. Saito.

2. **Uncertainty avoidance.** Defines how society deals with ambiguity. The higher the level of perceived ambiguity, the greater the need to reduce uncertainty. In Japan, Greece, and Portugal, details have to be clearly stated and all eventualities prepared for before proceeding with business. In other cultures, like Singapore, Denmark, or Sweden, there is less fear of uncertainty. For example, in many Asian companies, meetings are held to plan a future meeting. Here, lower-level managers agree to a business arrangement, but there will be a banquet that will be attended by top executives who sign or ratify the formal agreement. Also, buyers from certain cultures are reluctant to change suppliers until they are convinced the new partner is trustworthy and dependable.

3. **Individualism/Collectivism.** Means that some cultures are more group oriented than others in their decision process. For example, in the U.S., individualism is a

major part of one's culture. Think about the prominence of business leaders like Donald Trump® and Martha Stewart® in the U.S. But in other countries, especially in Asia, group cohesion and safety are important aspects of all business decisions. No one will make a decision until the group has been consulted and a consensus is reached. There is an old Japanese saying, "The nail that sticks up gets hammered down," that provides insight about individualism in that culture. Buyers from cultures that rate high in collectivism are offended by "hard closing" salespersons.

4. **Masculinity/Femininity.** Describes the traits valued by a society. Masculine traits that are seen include strength, success, and confidence. Feminine traits encompass nurturing, building relationships, and improving one's quality of life. In masculine cultures, individuals view wealth building as a primary goal. This trait is less important in feminine cultures. Buyers from masculine cultures tend to be more responsive to financial approaches than customers from feminine cultures.

5. **Confucian dynamism.** Focuses on time differences. Cultures that rate high on Confucian dynamism are primarily Asian and focus on the long-term and value commitment and persistence. For example, firms in the U.S. often focus on short-term time periods like the current quarter or calendar year for sales and profits. In Japan, goals and views tend to be more long-term. In one Japanese firm, managers were asked to prepare a 1,000-year plan. Gaining trust and forming relationships does not occur overnight in cultures that rank high on Confucian dynamism.

Local culture, found in rural areas, cities, and neighborhoods, can also influence customer behavior. Clothing and hair styles, diet, slang, and religious practices are influenced by local culture. Although local cultures exist, they are less influential on business buying decisions than national culture. The salesperson should cautiously adopt local culture, like slang or dress, because of the possibility of being perceived by the buyer as being insincere.

CULTURAL COMPONENTS

To understand culture, there are eight components a salesperson should consider before engaging in buyer-seller meetings.

1. **Communication**
2. **Religion**
3. **Education**
4. **Aesthetics**
5. **Social Organizations**
6. **Technology**
7. **Time**
8. **Values and Norms**

COMMUNICATION

A major area of cultural conflict can be attributed to ineffective communications. To be understood, words and phrases must be clearly communicated. The receiver of the message—the potential buyer—translates words into signs and symbols based upon their *cultural* understanding of what was said. Thus, language allows ideas to be transmitted between the buyer and the seller.

Problems with communication are sure to occur unless the sender of the message understands the receiver's culture.

How people communicate varies widely within and between cultures. Across cultures, words and phrases are utilized differently. In certain cultures, like the Philippines, "yes" can mean anything from "Yes, I will consider your product" to "Yes, I hear you." Also, members of certain sub-cultures may speak more loudly or with more emotion. Think about animated discussions between African-, Jewish-, or Italian-Americans. Other Americans may view these discussions as a sign of hostility or assertiveness, whereas these cultural groups appear to view their discussions as exciting conversation between friends.[1]

Cross-Cultural Communication Problems

A number of common communication problems complicate cross-cultural interactions: carelessness, multiple-meaning words, idioms, and slang. *Carelessness* occurs when the salesperson is not properly prepared and speaks extemporaneously—almost ensuring the likelihood of misspeaking. That is, an unprepared salesperson uses a word not understood by the customer or makes insensitive remarks. Words can also have *multiple meanings* in different cultures (e.g., the motor *runs* smoothly). And, a word used in the U.S. can offend someone from another culture (e.g., this is a "*bad-ass*" machine). *Idioms* are words that have no literal translation. If a salesperson were to say, "Our product is the Cadillac of the industry," "It is raining cats and dogs," or "I'm under the weather," such phrases would have no translatable meaning to someone from another culture. Likewise, "comparing apples and oranges" is a common sales metaphor that might be translated literally by a buyer who has yet to master the American lexicon. Lastly, there is *slang*. An example occurs when a buyer asks the seller, "What's the *damage* for the product?" meaning "How much does the product cost?" When salespersons employ careless words or use inappropriate words, idioms, or slang, *noise* is generated that reduces the efficiency of communication between individuals from different cultures.

Other differences that a salesperson must understand and consider when engaging in cross-cultural communications include

- **Tone of voice.** Refers to loudness, tone, and clarity of response. In certain sub-cultures, bargaining between buyer and seller are loud and emotional. Conversely, most Asian cultures perceive loud and emotional discussions to be inappropriate.

- **Timing of response.** Means the length of time one takes to consider the question asked. In the U.S., waiting too long to respond may be considered a sign of dishonesty; however, Asian cultures generally pause and reflect on an issue before responding.

- **Interruptions.** Asian cultures in general regard interruptions to be rude, while French, Italian, and Middle Eastern cultures are comfortable when multiple persons talk at once and interrupt at will.

- **Degree of directness.** Asians, Hispanics, and East Indians soften negative responses. Japanese buyers may ask a question rather than answer "no." Most mainline Americans believe that business discussions should be direct, no-holds-barred discussions.

- **Degree of embellishment.** Italian or Middle Eastern cultures make flowery, embellished statements as an artistic form of expression.

A key when communicating with someone who has been accul-turated or raised in another culture is to *not* breach the rules of etiquette. In such circumstances, it is best for the seller to mir-ror the buyer's communications behavior. If the buyer speaks slowly, does not interrupt, is less direct, and does not embellish, the seller should adapt their presentation to the communication pattern of the buyer.

Also, cross-cultural communications can differ depending upon the directness of the words. In *low-context* cultures, like the U.S., words are used exclusively to communicate what is meant. If something is not said, the receiver of the message does not necessarily assume that they should read between the lines. In *high-context* cultures, however, the opposite is true. That is, in high-context cultures, like those found in most Asian and Middle Eastern cultures, many details and specifics are left unsaid, and the receiver gains insight through non-verbal communications.

When humans communicate non-verbally, what is not stated is often as, or more, important than what is orally communi-cated. Therefore, non-verbal communications are important for both the buyer and seller and include:

- **Appearance.** Different cultures have distinct expecta-tions about facial hair and attire that includes formality of dress—Europeans tend to dress more formally than Americans.

- **Posture.** Involves sitting, standing, and offering some-one a seat. In Asian culture, a person of lesser status does not tower over or turn their back on a superior. In low power distance societies, like Scandinavia, such actions are viewed to be less important.

- **Space/Distance.** The physical distance between the cus-tomer and the salesperson. Americans generally prefer a larger "zone of comfort" around their body than do Latin Americans. Middle Eastern males and Hispanics operate in spaces of 0–18 inches; mainstream Americans and Western Europeans feel comfortable in zones of 18 inches to three feet; Asians generally prefer space of three feet or greater.

- **Sense of smell.** Includes body odors and colognes/perfumes. In certain cultures, strong body odor is accepted; but in other cultures, body odors are viewed as being offensive.

- **Hand gestures.** Can mean something other than intended—the "OK" sign in the U.S. is considered offensive in most European nations. Use of the left hand is not recommended when conducting business or eating with Moslem and Hindu buyers.

- **Handshakes.** Americans provide a firm handshake in comparison to a soft handshake by the British and a frequently repeated, moderate grasp by Hispanics.

- **Physical contact.** In Spanish cultures, friends touch constantly, but in most Asian nations, touching is seldom observed, and almost never on the head.

- **Eye contact.** Prolonged or direct eye contact is considered aggressive in some cultures, while it is a sign of honesty in other nations.

- **Body angles.** Refers to how one is positioned in relation to others. For example, in Japan, the person with the least status, such as the salesperson, bows lower than the customer. One should never turn their back on a superior in Asia.

Non-verbal signals between the buyer and the seller are helpful in determining what has been communicated. Unfortunately, body language is not universal around the world. Eye contact is a good example of how body language can be confusing. For example, when speaking with a buyer from Asia, it may be that the person is either (1) not understanding what is being said or (2) showing respect by not making direct eye contact with the seller. Also, beware of continual nodding and smiling that is out of sequence with your presentation. One cross-cultural communications expert recommends looking for the following non-verbal signs that suggest the buyer is less than clear about what the seller is saying.

- **A lack of interruptions.** No interruptions may mean the message is not being understood.

- **Efforts to change the subject.** If the listener does not understand, they may try to change the subject.

- **Absence of questions.** It may be that the listener does not understand and is unable to compose a question.

- **Inappropriate laughter.** Laughter may be a sign of poor comprehension and embarrassment rather than disrespect.

- **Allow time for questions.** Non-native listeners may need more time to compose questions.

- **Beware of "yes" answers.** Especially in Asia, "yes" may mean "Yes, I hear you," rather than "Yes, I understand."

- **Beware of a positive response to a negative question.** Asian buyers may say "yes" when asked if they understand. What they are doing is agreeing with the question.

- **Ask the listener to repeat what you have said.** This should only be done in private and you should be suspicious when the buyer repeats verbatim without demonstrating a real understanding of what has been said.

Based upon: Sondra Thiederman (1991), *Bridging Cultural Barriers for Corporate Success*, Lexington, MA: Lexington Books, pp. 67-69.

There is little doubt that the better informed and educated a salesperson is about verbal and non-verbal customer communications, the less likely a mistake will be made. The goal in all sales encounters is to *avoid* words or actions the customer might perceive to be offensive or inappropriate. Once you offend a customer, no matter how unintentional, it can be very difficult and expensive to repair the damage. Also, non-verbal communication missteps reduce the likelihood that negotiators will accurately understand their similarities and differences.[2] Finally, by understanding non-verbal communications, the seller can not only better comprehend what the buyer says, but also what they mean.

RELIGION

Religious beliefs have an important bearing on personal actions. One's religious beliefs influence what one drinks and eats, the hours or days available for work, and how one interacts with salespersons, co-workers, and members of the opposite gender. This means that a Moslem or Jewish customer observes or celebrates different holidays than Christian salespersons. Always be careful when trying to politely recognize these observations. For example, one well-intentioned Christian salesperson sent a *Kwanza* card to a Jewish buyer, unintentionally trying to acknowledge *Chanukah.* Customers that strictly observe cultural dietary laws, such as kosher or vegetarianism, might hesitate to accept an invitation to a meal for fear that something about the food will violate their beliefs. Salespersons should select restaurants carefully, since even "kosher" delis may not qualify if dairy products are served with meat or if ham is offered on the menu. Although it is customary to give gifts to customers during holidays, remember that leather products are strictly taboo for Hindu-observant customers, and it's not prudent to offer a bottle of wine or whiskey to a Moslem buyer for any occasion.

EDUCATION

In some cultures, it is difficult for a salesperson to be accepted unless they possess a similar level of education as the customer. Education, social class, and occupation are mutually intertwined in most cultures.[3] Customers from certain cultural backgrounds expect their salesperson to be equally educated so that complex issues can be discussed and potential solutions can be offered. For example, a German-born researcher at a prestigious institution refused to speak with salespeople that did not possess a Ph.D. in chemistry. This is because in many cultures a comparable level of education infers that the person has equal status and is knowledgeable of correct social behavior. Likewise, if your buyer earned an engineering or business degree, it will be easier to discuss technical specifications and cost-benefit analysis. If you sell to cross-cultural customers you should consider earning a certified sales designation and ensure that your degree (M.B.A, B.S. in Engineering)—if it is relevant—and certification are clearly displayed on your business cards.

AESTHETICS

Each culture perceives different objects to be beautiful and visually appealing. How one dresses, how artwork is appreciated, and how food is presented are impacted by one's culture. If a salesperson is asked to make a sales presentation or develop sales promotional materials, cultural aesthetics like colors and shapes should be carefully considered. For example, several U.S. firms placed Arabic writing and the flag of Saudi Arabia on products and advertisements only to learn that *Allah* had been blasphemed. Colors, styles, and shapes must be carefully considered before making a presentation or printing proposals that could offend the potential customer. In Asian countries,

EXHIBIT 3-1
Cultural Significance of Colors in Asia

Color	Significance	Culture(s)
Red	Joy and Happiness	China and Japan
Purple	Associated with heaven/emperor	China
Blue	Funeral color (ultramarine)	China
Green	Health, growth, prosperity	China
Yellow/ Gold	Wealth and Authority	China
White	Funeral color	Most Asian nations
Black	Guilt, unlucky, death	India

as seen in Exhibit 3-1, white is the primary funeral color, while gold and yellow colors connote wealth, authority, and longevity.[4] Surprisingly, seeing one's name in red ink is associated with being deceased and can cause Asian-born buyers to withdraw from a business transaction.[5]

SOCIAL ORGANIZATIONS

Social organizations include the groups the individual belongs to in a society. These associations include family, community groups, special interest groups, and work groups. Again, groups are most important in cultures that have a high collectivism rating. Difficulties can also arise when a salesperson from a blue-collar area calls upon primarily white-collar customers. When this happens, the words used and social graces employed can severely strain a potential working relationship. Buyers from certain cultures will only purchase from salespersons that have been accepted into the buyer's inner circle. Although a caste system is not officially recognized in North America, more than one sale has been lost because the buyer did not deem the salesperson to be socially worthy of the order.

TECHNOLOGY

It is important for the salesperson to understand the technological sophistication and limitations of potential customers. In many situations today, engineers who occupy technical positions within global firms have emigrated from other nations. To improve the chances of sales success, it is important for salespersons to possess at least a similar level of technological expertise as the customer. An example of this might be a computer salesperson that has less expertise about computers than the engineer buyer they are calling upon.

Moreover, some cultures favor hard work over modern conveniences, and the introduction of technically advanced products may be viewed as unnecessary luxuries. Many immigrants from Asian or Eastern European countries expect to work long, hard hours to succeed and are not impressed by fancy electronics or automation. When introduced to the price-scanning device, one Hungarian-born merchant responded indignantly to the enthusiastic salesman, "Come back when I can't read the price tags anymore."

TIME

The concept of time also varies by culture. Some cultures focus on the past (talk about history, family origin, business, and nation); others focus on the present (activities and enjoyment of the moment); and still other cultures focus on the future (talk of prospects, aspirations, and future achievement). Salespersons can use time values to emphasize the history, tradition, or cultural heritage as evidence of potential for past- and present-oriented firms. Likewise, emphasizing the opportunity for future greatness works well with future-oriented buyers.

The observation of time also varies by culture. In modern cultures with efficient transportation systems, it is important to arrive promptly for appointed meetings. Otherwise, this cultural affront may be difficult to overcome. However, in less developed cultures, time is viewed more relatively. The customer is less concerned about time, and the salesperson must be adaptable and understanding when the customer forgets appointments or arrives at the office late. For example, when arriving early for an appointment with a Guatemalan-born customer, a salesperson was surprised to learn that her buyer was still out for lunch and wasn't expected back for at least half an hour.

This component of culture can also include the time period in getting to know the customer, learning to trust one another, and making purchase decisions. Female Hispanic business owners, for example, take a longer time period to make decisions, so the salesperson must be patient and wait. Because minorities take longer to make decisions, salespersons may need to make additional calls on minority decision-makers before attempting to close,[6] which can provide new leads since minorities tend to pass on more referrals. Also, Italian business managers are likely to spend considerable time on small talk at sales meetings, whereas Scandinavians prefer a short, formal introduction that is immediately followed by business discussion.[7]

VALUES AND NORMS

Members of a culture set rules or standards of acceptable and unacceptable behavior.[8] Some major cultural *rules,* or *norms,* include:
- Hard work as opposed to relaxation or leisure
- Egalitarian as compared to patriarchal decision-making
- Conservatism in contrast to liberalism
- Female submissiveness versus female liberation
- Ethnocentrism as opposed to polycentrism
- Youthfulness in contrast to maturity

Salespersons must be sensitive to the distinct values and norms practiced by buyers from different cultures. In general, a number of cultures view female salespersons as being less credible. This means that customers from the Middle East or certain Asian cultures may have more difficulty interacting with female sales representatives. In Japan, there is a saying: "Women are like the air, absolutely essential, but they should remain invisible."

Citizens of certain cultures view their way of doing business as being the only way (ethnocentrism) rather than one of many ways (polycentrism) of conducting commerce. Buyers and sellers who are *ethnocentric* may be more rigid, while those who are *polycentric* are more likely to be flexible in their business dealings. A form of *ethnocentrism* also exists within very large firms where sellers are expected to adopt the "Wal-Mart®" or "General Motors®" way of doing things.

ETHNOCENTRISM

Ethnocentrism has many meanings that suggest that other cultures should think, act, and behave as we do *or* they are going about things in the wrong way. Many mainline Americans interpret the actions of others through their own cultural lens of ethnocentrism. Thus, it is important for us to acknowledge that we must understand ourselves in order to truly come to know other cultures.

One major problem caused by ethnocentrism occurs when we try to interpret the actions of others in the context of our own culture. Mainline American culture suggests that someone who is being untruthful will not look the other person directly in the eyes. However, in many Asian cultures, looking at someone directly in the eyes for an extended period is believed to be disrespectful. When we evaluate the behavior of others based upon what we know, we use a *self-reference criterion.* The self-reference criterion through which we evaluate others is composed of our customs, institutions, and ways of thinking. Thus, we evaluate others based upon what we have learned and come to believe is true in our culture.

There is certainly nothing wrong in preferring our own cultural practices, but potential problems arise when we distort what we see in our relations with others. This is especially true for salespersons who are calling upon buyers who are products of other cultures and, as a result of our ethnocentrism, we misinterpret what is said or left unsaid. For example, in the U.S. it is considered "normal" to become friends quickly and share intimate details of our lives with our new friends. In other cultures, however, friendships are formed very slowly and attempting to form a new friendship so casually is viewed as being frivolous or even rude.

So, given that clinging to our ethnocentric views can lead to trouble, why do we continue to gauge the actions of others through our tinted glasses? There are several explanations for this human behavior. First, it is comforting to believe we can understand the behavior of others by comparing those behaviors to values we trust and cherish. Second, if we admit our views are not universal, we also acknowledge there is more we need to learn about others. Finally, this leads to a conclusion that our methods of coping do not work in a culturally diverse marketplace.

How does one overcome ethnocentrism? The first way to reduce ethnocentrism is to learn about other cultures. You are doing this right now by reading and studying this book. You are learning to recognize and understand the values that motivate people from different cultures to behave the way they do. With this knowledge, it becomes easier to apply what you have learned to future sales situations you encounter. This awareness allows you to understand why an Asian- or African-American buyer takes longer to form a relationship instead of prematurely dismissing the potential customer as someone who is not ready to commit to a relationship with you and your company.

The second way to overcome ethnocentrism is to become

more aware of the beliefs that can distort your perceptions and cause you to misinterpret your customers. In effect, learning about your own cultural beliefs allows you to compensate for incorrectly analyzing behavior influenced by another culture.

One way to minimize the impact of ethnocentrism is to offer an apology at the beginning of the sales meeting. For example, a salesperson might say, "Thank you, Mr. Saito, for seeing me. I know that an important person like you is extremely busy. Should I say or do something that offends you, I ask your forgiveness in advance." Both authors have observed such behavior in different parts of the world in an effort to neutralize cultural *faux pas* that may occur during cross-cultural meetings. One business person from the Middle East always apologized as he was departing. Either way, this tactic allows the salesperson to communicate to the buyer that any perceived cultural blunders were unintentional. This must be done carefully, and with full sincerity, or it might be perceived as being patronizing and condescending.

Although mainline Americans believe that the U.S. is simply a mixture of all the immigrants that came to this geographical location over the past four centuries, let's examine a few proverbs taught in the U.S. Proverbs have been described as the "essence of a culture."[9] Numerous proverbs are well known in American culture and a few of these are listed below.

- *The early bird gets the worm.*
- *There is no fool like an old fool.*
- *The sweetest grapes hang the highest in the tree.*
- *If at first you don't succeed, try, try again.*
- *Take the bull by the horns.*

Now, let's consider what these proverbs teach us. The early bird gets the worm because he rises early to begin work. The second proverb, regarding an old fool, suggests youthfulness is more important than being elderly. Sweet grapes that hang high require additional work to gather, so this proverb teaches us that to receive the best rewards requires a higher-level performance. Through perseverance, the fourth proverb urges us to not give up when things get difficult. Lastly, when we take the bull by the horns, we are taking initiative.

If we focus on just these five proverbs, we can gain an insightful view of mainline United States culture. That is, U.S. culture tends to focus on youthfulness, arising early, performing additional work, not giving up when our efforts are met with resistance, and taking individual initiative to make things happen. But we must remember that proverbs differ markedly in other cultures. In traditional Philippine culture, prior to marriage, children are expected to find all adults in the house at dusk and demonstrate appropriate honor by placing the adult's hand on their forehead.[10] Elders in many societies of the world are shown reverence by younger people. There is also a Chinese proverb that says the duck that flies too far out front gets shot down. This means that it is better to fly in a group than to try to get out in front of one's colleagues. As we have stated throughout this book, in most Asian cultures, there is a leaning toward collectivistic actions and it is unlikely someone from China or Asia who is a B2B buyer is going to take initiative, unless he is told to do so by his boss. In the Middle East, rather than trying repeatedly to succeed, the buyer may decide that divine intervention has determined that the individual should not succeed. If God, who controls all things, does not want someone to succeed, what can a humble human being do?

Bridging barriers between cultural differences is among the most difficult lessons to learn. Learning about *stereotypes* in Chapter 1 and now *ethnocentrism* allows the salesperson to succeed cross-culturally by (1) viewing the buyer as an individual rather than a caricature and (2) understanding that our own cultural beliefs tint how we view our interactions with others. By better understanding ourselves and others, we can be ourselves, communicate respect for our buyers and others, and make reasonable compromises. Even when we interact with buyers from other geographical areas of the U.S., we must engage in these same actions. Our previous experiences working with buyers in other parts of the U.S. places us on the road to successfully interacting with buyers and professionals raised in other cultures.

SUMMARY

Culture influences the behaviors and expectations of all humans. That is, culture shapes what we see, how we make sense of these views, and how we express ourselves in response. When salespersons understand the nature of culture and how it is manifested, they can adapt their behaviors to increase the probability of successful interaction with buyers from different cultures. This means that the more knowledgeable you are about culture, the easier it will be to respect and accept the diversity that increases each year in the U.S. Cultural knowledge also decreases ethnocentrism, or the belief by most cultures that the way they think, believe, and approach problems is the only way of behaving. By recognizing and understanding the effect of ethnocentrism, salespersons can practice cultural sensitivity in their communications and interactions so as to enhance the likelihood of building long-term relationships with customers. Finally, remember that business relationships are based upon trust. Unless buyers and sellers respect and understand one another's culture, how can they come to trust one another?

CHAPTER 3 TAKE-AWAY POINTS:

- Culture is learned from the family and society in which we are born and raised.

- People from different cultures do not necessarily share the same ways of thinking, feeling, or behaving.

- Potential problems arise in sales situations when cultural components are unknown or misunderstood.

- Human behavior is influenced by global, national, and local cultures.

- National culture is the most important cultural level and comprises five components:

    Power distance. Acceptance of unequal power distribution.

    Uncertainty avoidance. How ambiguity is viewed and practiced.

    Individualism/Collectivism. The degree of individual or group orientation.

    Masculinity/Femininity. The traits valued by society.

    Confucian dynamism. The culture's long- vs. short-term view of the world.

- Cultural components consist of communication, religion, education, aesthetics, social organizations, technology, time, and values and norms.

- When cultures view their way as the only way of behaving, they are *ethnocentric*.

- By understanding *ethnocentrism*, salespersons come to see that they are judging the actions of others through their cultural lens.

- Clinging to ethnocentrism causes us to misjudge why our buyers behave the way they do.

- Conversely, cultures that accept more than one way to conduct business practice a *polycentric* approach.

4

HOW TO SELL CROSS-CULTURALLY

Nearly all salespersons learn a selling process that encompasses a series of steps beginning with searching for customers and ending with actually closing the sale. In this chapter, a cross-cultural sales process is introduced that includes the following seven steps:

1. **Finding Customers**
2. **Preparing**
3. **Relationship Building**
4. **Product Offering**
5. **Offer Clarification**
6. **Securing the Purchase**
7. **Maintaining the Relationship**

The purpose of a sales process is to organize the activities a salesperson engages in while performing their job. Do not confuse the steps taught with a rigid, prescriptive process that one must blindly follow. If anything, selling cross-culturally means being infinitely familiar with the sales process, while making adaptations at every step of the process. Each of the seven steps, with a focus on cultural influences, is now discussed.

FINDING CUSTOMERS

Most salespersons have to identify and investigate potential customers to ensure they are worthy of additional effort being invested in order to convert them to customer status. Normally, potential customer lists are large, but actual customer lists are much smaller. Salespersons have many methods from which to choose for finding potential customers.

- **Internal Sources.** Company records, telemarketing leads, service department, and surveys

- **External Sources.** Satisfied customers, networking, friends, swap meets, and directories

- **Promotional Sources.** Contests, direct mail, trade shows, and educational seminars

- **Personal Actions.** Cold calling, purchase cycle, orphan adoption, and paid referrals

A few methods for finding new customers are greatly impacted by culture. Beginning with external sources, buyers from distinct cultures will view the act of sharing information about friends quite differently than the salesperson. They may ask, "Why would someone provide information about friends or business associates to a salesperson?" Likewise, receiving letters, direct mail, or attending an educational seminar may be misperceived by the potential buyer. In many cultures, strangers do not send anonymous mail asking people to meet with them and purchase a product. Thus, direct mail will likely be viewed with skepticism. In the B2B environment, traditional methods of calling upon designated buyers of goods and requests for quotations remain the same.

In regard to qualifying the potential customer, four conditions come into play: money, authority, need, and fit. First, does the potential customer possess the economic resources or credit to purchase your product? Second, can the buyer legally sign for the purchase? Third, does the buyer actually need or want the product? And, fourth, is there "fit" or compatibility between the buyer's organization and that of the seller? Perhaps the buyer's firm only purchases the lowest priced product and you know your company will not offer the lowest price. If the potential customer does not satisfy each of these conditions, you are probably wasting both your time and that of the buyer. Given that most B2B sales calls in the U.S. cost $150–200 to make, salespersons cannot afford to engage in unproductive sales calls with unlikely customers.

PREPARING

Successful salespersons spend significant time preparing for meetings with potential customers. This includes learning about the potential buyer's culture, organization, product line(s), competitors, and past relationships. In today's competitive marketplace, the average salesperson must make four to five sales calls prior to closing a sale. When dealing with a cross-cultural buyer, it will likely mean that a greater number of visits are necessary before a relationship is established.

Prior to meeting with the potential buyer, make sure you can correctly pronounce the buyer's name—if necessary, call the company and speak with a receptionist. Check an Internet search engine to see if the buyer's name exists on a website. This may provide you with information about the buyer's hobbies, part-time businesses, social organizations, or religious affiliations. Any information you can gather about the buyer—from existing company files or customer relationship management systems may be helpful in future meetings. Also, based upon your research of the firm, try to anticipate product needs and how your product/service best satisfies those needs. Finally, make sure you understand the advantages your products offer over those of your competitors.

If you are making a formal presentation, now is the time to carefully select colors and words carefully for transparencies and PowerPoint presentations. When possible, seek feedback or advice from your sales manager, trusted colleagues, and technical staff. In regard to your business card, be sure that colors—such as red—are not utilized. If the buyer speaks English as a second language, you should seriously consider having dual-language business cards printed. Such detailed planning and preparation should be repeated for all future meetings. One pharmaceutical sales manager told the authors, "Pre-call planning is 'the key' to making great calls and achieving success."

RELATIONSHIP BUILDING

In the initial meeting, it is essential to make a favorable impression and begin to gain the trust of the potential customer. In some cultures, where relationships are based upon utility or common advantage, relationship building proceeds more quickly, while in other cultures it takes longer to establish a relationship. There are a number of ways to meet a prospect.

- **Guaranteed introduction.** Meeting the prospect in the presence of a trusted friend who speaks positively of each party and serves as a reference or guarantor.

- **Referral introduction.** Informing the potential customer that a mutual friend has given their name and asked that you call upon them.

- **Personal introduction.** Personally introducing yourself and exchanging business cards. This is done in a ritualistic fashion in some cultures (e.g., Japan). It is advisable to keep your cards in your jacket pocket or in a formal business card holder rather than in your wallet. You should present your card with dignity and then wait for the buyer's card to be formally presented. Once you receive the buyer's card, pause and take time to seriously examine the card. Then say the buyer's name; if a mistake is made, ask the buyer to repeat his name until you achieve the correct pronunciation. Never write on the card for any reason—this can be a serious cultural affront!

- **Benefit introduction.** Introducing yourself and immediately asking the buyer if they would like to save money, time, or gain some benefit. This introduction is commonly utilized by salespersons in U.S. firms.

Cultures differ in how relationships are formed, but *trust* is an essential component of all relationships. An initial first step to trust is getting to know one another. As seen in one of the scenarios in this book, Spanish customers may want to spend time eating, drinking, and socializing prior to initiating business. Likewise, Asian buyers normally take long periods of time getting to know their suppliers. This may include golf outings where business is only discussed if initiated by the buyer. You should *never* underestimate the importance of building relationships with your potential customers (See Exhibit 4-1).

EXHIBIT 4-1

Building Relationships with Hispanic and Asian Buyers

Here are some tips for building relationships with Hispanic buyers.

- Only use Spanish in advertisements, handouts, or in person if you are fluent and know what you are doing. If not, then rely upon professionals to use the correct words in the proper context.

- Expect the entire family to be involved in the purchase. Family is of great importance to Hispanics, and you must be polite and respectful of family members, especially senior family members.

- Be formal in your dealings. Use Mr., Mrs., Sir, or Ma'am, rather than first names, unless told otherwise.

- Expect the buying process to take longer to complete. Hispanics prefer to form a relationship with merchants and service providers.

- Hispanics are more loyal and recommend firms that provide outstanding service to their friends, family, and neighbors. Thus, there is a payoff for making an extra effort to satisfy this cultural group.

Adapted from "Marketing to Hispanics," Delia Passi Smalter, www.advisortoday.com, December 2, 2004.

Here are some tips for building relationships with Asian buyers.

- Asian resistance to salespersons is greater than that of American customers.

- It is best not to probe too hard for facts or be too direct.

- Trust is very important; ethics are critical.

Continued on the following page.

- Asians are often reluctant to borrow, and when they say they cannot afford something, they are being honest. They are not playing games and neither should the salesperson.

- Ask polite questions in order to understand buyer background and perspectives.

- Always be sensitive and be yourself.

- If another approach is needed, then, by all means, change course.

Adapted from "The changing face of the insurance business," Eric Weissman, *Life Association News*, April 1993, 88:4, 46–54.

PRODUCT OFFERING

Sales presentations are both formal and informal in nature. In effect, the salesperson makes small sales presentations prior to the formal sales presentation that communicates the offer to the buyer. In every meeting, the seller is "selling" the benefits of the product, listening to concerns, allaying reservations through additional information, and adjusting the offer. When selling cross-culturally, it is important to ask more questions to establish buyer objectives than when selling to someone from your own culture.[1]

In most cultures, the salesperson should dress appropriately, smile, and make positive remarks about the buyer and his or her firm. In uncertainty-avoidance cultures, meetings are very formal, whereas in other cultures, meetings include food, talk, and banter. "Preliminaries" give both the buyer and seller an opportunity to share information and make sense of the other side's position. Cross-cultural sales calls tend to be lengthier, less structured, and involve give and take on the parts of both buyer and seller. It is naive to assume a slick sales presentation can be taught that maneuvers the buyer into having to purchase a product. This is especially true in B2B situations where buyers have multiple sellers who want to satisfy their needs. In B2B situations, high-pressure sales tactics are seldom successful.

In a cross-cultural setting, it is important to begin the sales presentation with a discussion of previous meetings and promises made by both parties. The salesperson should also reiterate the buyer's goals in regard to price, quality, reliability, and delivery. In this way, both the buyer and seller are certain they are entering the meeting from the same point. Once a situational need is identified, it is time for the salesperson to communicate "how" the product/service will create value for the buyer. This means the salesperson must be capable of discussing the area of concern, proposing solutions that benefit the customer in a way that is not offensive to the buyer. The salesperson's goal is to explain how the product/service satisfies the buyer's needs and furthers the buyer's goals.

OFFER CLARIFICATION

Once the sales presentation is completed, the salesperson should expect and welcome questions. Buyer concerns, clarification questions, and requests are normal in any sales situation. In effect, the buyer asks questions to clarify the seller's offer or ask for concessions. When engaged in this stage of the sales process, it is necessary for the salesperson to utilize their finely honed abilities of listening, reading body language, and looking for non-verbal hints that provide insight into the buyer's concerns.

This is also the time when test result data or samples are requested or offered. The buyer may also want to negotiate price concessions. Sellers should understand that selling on price alone is seldom a viable strategy. A better strategy is to discuss the total value provided by the product offering. Total value includes such attributes as the product, service, training, maintenance, warranty, and trade-in options. This is also the time when buyers and sellers negotiate about matters of importance. Always remember that negotiation is a two-way street (See Exhibit 4-2).

EXHIBIT 4-2
Improving Your Negotiation Skills

Frequent price discounts can have a negative impact on a product's value and profitability. When a buyer asks for a price concession, be prepared to ask for a concession from the buyer. That is, if the buyer wants a five-percent discount, then the salesperson should ask for a larger volume of shipments. Likewise, if the buyer asks for a product demonstration, the salesperson could ask that the decision maker be present for the event. Listed below are six pointers for improving your negotiation skills.

1. Before calling on the buyer, try to anticipate expected buyer concerns.
2. Ask questions that will uncover specific buyer needs.
3. Try to never give a unilateral concession; ask for something in return.
4. Rather than respond immediately and perhaps incorrectly, tell the buyer you will provide the information later.
5. Don't fold or agree to concessions too quickly.
6. Stay calm and friendly. Hostility seldom works in the seller's favor.

Adapted from "The Best Way to Negotiate," Sarah Lorge, *Sales and Marketing Management*, March 1998, 92.

SECURING THE PURCHASE

Many sales books and seminars advocate "closing techniques" that maneuver the buyer into agreeing to purchase a product or service. In most situations, and particularly in cross-cultural B2B settings, such high-pressure techniques seldom work. If they do work, a salesperson must ask, "How will trust and long-term relationships possibly be strengthened?" In most situations, once it is evident that the seller's goods meet the buyer's needs, the question is: since my offer meets your needs, should we do business?

Culture influences the buyer's decision styles. In Asian cultures, most decisions are made as part of a group consensus. A salesperson must wait for a consensus to be reached, no matter how long it takes. If the purchase decision is based primarily upon price, the decision to purchase occurs in a much shorter time period. Likewise, many cross-cultural buyers are reluctant to give up the comfort and security of an existing supplier. In order to convince the buyer to switch suppliers, the salesperson must convey trust and perseverance. Both actions take time to convey.

MAINTAINING THE RELATIONSHIP

Once the buyer purchases your product, the salesperson must work closely with the buying firm to answer questions, resolve problems, and represent the position of the buyer within the selling firm. To retain the buyer as a long-term customer, salespersons must deliver on all promises. At European firms, fast-talking, hard-selling salespersons will not survive. Similarly, in Japanese firms, suppliers must conform to exact product standards if they are to succeed.[2] Sales research has shown that it is easier and less costly to sell to a satisfied customer than to seek and convert an unknown account.

SUMMARY

The chapter presented a seven-step, cross-cultural sales process. Cultural forces impact all stages of the sales process. This means that salespersons who call upon customers from diverse cultures and backgrounds must master the flow of the sales process while adapting to each customer's distinctive needs. While it may not be possible to master any culture—even your own—the greater understanding you have of culture the greater the likelihood you will open your mind and heart to your customers' differences. This will lead to improved relationships, higher levels of trust, and a willingness on the part of both parties to seek "win-win" business deals.

CHAPTER 4 TAKE-AWAY POINTS:

- A sales process organizes the activities a salesperson engages in with the buyer.

- Selling cross-culturally means following a process, but adapting when necessary.

- The sales process can be described in seven steps:
  1. Finding Customers
  2. Preparing
  3. Relationship Building
  4. Product Offering
  5. Offer Clarification
  6. Securing the Purchase
  7. Maintaining the Relationship

- In cross-cultural selling, preparation is extremely important.

- Trust is an essential component of all relationships.

- Cross-cultural sales calls are lengthier and less structured.

- A salesperson should expect the buyer to raise questions and concerns, and ask for clarification.

- Negotiation is a two-way street that is to be expected.

- Culture impacts the buyer's decision style. Expect the decision to take longer.

- To retain the cross-cultural buyer, it is essential to deliver on all promises.

5

ACTUAL CULTURAL ENCOUNTERS

Another way to gain an understanding, while reinforcing how to sell cross-culturally, is to examine actual mistakes made by salespersons. In this chapter, eleven scenarios that encompass a wide variety of sales situations are presented. Poor communications, cultural blunders, age and status differences, nationalism, and sexual discrimination are explored in the mini case studies. After each scenario, the situation is analyzed and recommendations are made for achieving a successful cross-cultural encounter.

IT'S ALL ABOUT THE YIN-YANG

Sun Gil Kim was born in Seoul, Korea, and was educated at Rutgers University. After college, he returned to Korea and worked for a large Korean electronics firm. Most recently, he was assigned to a management position in North Carolina, where he is responsible for the assembly of computer parts. Gerry Henderson sells robotic soldering devices and is calling on Mr. Kim.

> **Gerry:** *Hello, Mr. Kim?*
> **Kim:** *Yes?*

Gerry: *Hi. I'm Gerry Henderson from Autoflux. Got a few minutes?*

Kim: *I'm pretty busy. Maybe later.*

Gerry: *I think it would be worth your time to know about our fine soldering products.*

Kim: *I hear of Autoflux. It is my job to know.*

Gerry: *Great! Then you must be interested in our new Jet-Set high-speed system.*

Kim: *No, I have very little interest in automation. We work two shifts, and I ensure that the work is done with minimum defects.*

Gerry: *But you can work much more efficiently with the Jet-Set. It will probably get as much done in one shift that you now do in two.*

Kim: *Yes, but I like how things are. I have good workers and they produce good work.*

Gerry: *I understand, but don't you want to increase your output?*

Kim: *We meet the output requirements of our company. Our assembly output depends on parts availability. The parts come from Korea. I am assigned to keep a balance of incoming parts with outgoing boards. No more, no less.*

Gerry: *But here's your chance to be a hero to the boys in Korea. You can get them working harder to get you more of the parts you need.*

Kim: *I don't think so. I'm afraid that's not my place to put pressure on my company to work harder.*

Gerry: *Yeah, but don't you want to impress your boss?*

Kim: *What do you mean? What has that to do with my job?*

> **Gerry:** *You know. More output should open some eyes to your ability to make the big decisions.*
>
> **Kim:** *I'm afraid my time is up. Now please excuse me.*

Unfortunately, Gerry and Mr. Kim have just had a major cultural misunderstanding. Gerry makes the incorrect assumption that Mr. Kim, who was actually raised in Korea, is concerned with the U.S. values of efficiency and individualism. Mr. Kim's goal is meeting the requirements set by his Korean executives. It appears from the scenario that Mr. Kim needs to produce high-quality products on time. Since increasing output has not been requested by the executives in Seoul, it would be inappropriate for Mr. Kim to raise this topic with his superiors.

Gerry needs to first understand that doing business with an Asian customer will take much longer than it would with U.S. or Canadian customers. Doing business with someone from an Asian culture generally means that long periods of time are needed to get to know the supplier and learn if they are honorable and can be trusted. Perhaps Gerry uses an increased efficiency approach with his U.S. customers, but Mr. Kim clearly states that this is not one of his goals. Instead of listening and adjusting his sales approach to meet the customer's objective(s), Gerry then shifts to the strategy of how increasing efficiency can raise Kim's status in the eyes of his boss.

In most Korean firms, decisions are made at the top of the *chaebol* or industrial firm. Lower-level managers do not make decisions; they carry them out. Meeting quality and manufacturing standards and complying with directions are ways to maintain the boss's approval. Secondly, in most Asian nations, the "nail that sticks up gets hammered down." This means that managers do not want to appear different; they want to be viewed as team players. Therefore, both of Gerry's approaches are misguided given the cultural dynamics that exist.

To succeed, Gerry must invest time in Mr. Kim. This means he should take Mr. Kim to lunch at the location of his choice. Who knows? Mr. Kim may like to eat at Outback Steak House®. Initial discussions should focus on getting to know one another. In getting to know Mr. Kim, Gerry will slowly understand how he can be of service to this client. It is only when Mr. Kim feels he can trust Gerry that he will discuss his true needs. Gerry's approach has to be slow and service-oriented. Perhaps the best Gerry can hope for is to have Mr. Kim introduce him to a decision-maker when he next visits the local plant. In any future meeting, Gerry must focus on how his product will increase quality and ensure production goals are met. As a result of Mr. Kim's inability to purchase this product, this account must be viewed as long-term development. This may mean that Autoflux must contact the North American manager of the Korean electronics firm. Given the limited information provided in the case, it is unlikely that this account will result in a quick purchase based upon production efficiency.

UNO, DOS, TRES...NO SALE!

Richard Adams is calling on Raul Guzman for the first time. Raul was born in Mexico City and has lived in the Washington, D.C., area for the past six years. Richard graduated from Dartmouth College with a degree in economics.

> **Raul:** *Hello, Richard. Welcome! I'm Raul.* (Big smile and embracing handshake)
>
> **Richard:** *Hello, Mr. Guzman. Nice to meet you.*
>
> **Raul:** *Sit down and make yourself comfortable. Coffee? Soft drink?*

Richard: *No, thanks. I don't want to take up too much of your time.*

Raul: *No need to rush. How was your drive over here?*

Richard: *Fine. I want to get into your requirements for a new communications system. Can I ask you a few questions? It will only take a few minutes.*

Raul: *No problem,* amigo. *Ask away. Sure you don't want coffee?*

Richard: *No. I mean yes, I'm sure. How many people will be using the system?*

Raul: *Let's see. There's Joanne, Sammy, probably Cindy, maybe Stan, and…oh yeah, me.*

Richard: *That's three for sure and two maybes?*

Raul: *Whatever. We just want a system that is flexible.*

Richard: *That is somewhat vague. Could you be a little more specific?*

Raul: *What's so vague about flexible? I don't see any problem with that.*

Richard: *How can I recommend a system if I don't know how many people will be using it?*

Raul: *Okay. Let's say four or five, give or take one or two.*

Richard: *That could be two, three, four, five, six, or seven.*

Raul: *Right.* No problemo.

Richard: *Mr. Guzman, I think we are wasting each other's time. Call me when you have a definite number.*

Raul: *Are you sure you don't want a soft drink, Ricky?*

Once again, cultural misunderstanding has crept into the sales encounter. Raul, who hails from a culture that values friendship and stresses social interaction, appears to be less concerned with precision. He simply wants a system that fits his needs now and will adjust in the future. Richard, on the other hand, was trained as an economist and appears to feel that there is a precise answer for every situation.

From a cultural perspective, Richard has made a major mistake by not accepting Raul's hospitality. Spending time now in establishing a relationship, by having a soft drink and getting to know Raul, will pay dividends in the future. Richard's role is to help Raul solve his problem, and if Raul wants a flexible system, then that is what he should be offered. Why not design a system that will accommodate five people now, but can be expanded, as needed, in the future? Why does Richard believe that Raul should know precisely how many workers would be using the system? Perhaps the answer depends upon future sales or numbers of customers—information that Raul knows is less than accurate.

If Richard wants to succeed with Raul, he must modify his behavior. He must spend as much time as is necessary to establish a relationship. If Raul offers refreshments, Richard should accept even if the refreshment is not desired. Richard should not decline the offer. He can sip the drink and demonstrably thank Raul for his hospitality. Finally, if Raul is not certain how many people will utilize the new system, Richard must devise a plan that covers all situations within reason. It is the role of the salesperson to find a way to satisfy customer needs.

TUNG TIED

Mr. John Tung is a Taiwanese owner of a large camera store. He is being visited by Pete Stone of the Bigshot Equipment Company. This is Stone's initial attempt to sell to Mr. Tung.

Tung: *Welcome to Pics-R-Us, Mr. Stone.*

Stone: *Thank you, Mr. Tung. It's nice to meet you.*

Tung: *So what have you got to show me?*

Stone: *I have a new line of special camera accessories.*

Tung: *Oh? Let's have a look.*

(Stone hands Mr. Tung a tripod.)

Tung: *What makes it so special?*

Stone: *It is ultra lightweight. And, you'll be happy to know that it's made in China.*

Tung: *Why should that make me happy?*

Stone: *Aren't you from China?*

Tung: *I'm from Taiwan.*

Stone: *Right. Isn't that part of China?*

Tung: (shakes head) *Not exactly.*

Stone: *So you're from Taiwan, huh? Wow, I love Thai food. How about I take you to lunch at my favorite Thai restaurant?*

Tung: *I actually prefer Italian food, and I'm not very hungry right now. Thank you for your time.*

Stone demonstrates a lack of understanding of his customer and an ignorance of history and politics of China, which is the largest populated country in the world. Members of the

Nationalist Kuomintang Party fled to the island province of Taiwan in 1949 and established Nationalist China. For more than 50 years, the mainland People's Republic of China has threatened to reunite Taiwan by force. To confuse Taiwan with Beijing is a huge *faux pas*. Stone also demonstrates his lack of geographical knowledge when he suggests that Mr. Tung accompany him to a Thai restaurant. Both Taiwan and Thailand are in Asia, but their cultures, histories, and people are unique.

This scenario suggests that Mr. Stone needs to take more time to get to know Mr. Tung. Rather than launch into a demonstration of the product, he should devote time to getting to know Mr. Tung. Mr. Stone should also ask himself why he would think a customer might buy a product because it was made in their country of birth. Such a connection could be a positive factor, but few business people would purchase a product unless it was also superior in quality and performance. Even more important, Mr. Tung must sell the product to his customers who may prefer a certain product brand.

Stone should ask more questions of Mr. Tung as they get to know one another. If he has not traveled to Asia, he might ask Mr. Tung about his home. Such questions as "Where did you live prior to Chicago?" express genuine interest by telling the customer that you are less familiar with Taiwan than you would like, but you have heard it is a beautiful place. Perhaps Mr. Tung would suggest a locale that you should visit when you do get a chance to travel there.

Salespersons must be prepared prior to making the sales call. It is best to know as much as possible about the potential customer. If this is not possible, then do not make any leaps of logic about a person's home country. Keep your comments to the product and situation at hand. Mr. Stone should have discussed the merits of his product without interjecting the comment regarding China. Further damage was done when

Stone suggested they go to a Thai restaurant. Stone was unprepared and made careless remarks that hurt his chances of making a sale to Mr. Tung.

RUSSIAN ROULETTE

Michael Tuvinov defected to the United States from Moscow in 1984, prior to the demise of the U.S.S.R. He has a Ph.D. in chemistry and was hired as a research scientist for a large pharmaceutical company. Joe Sharillo is calling on Michael to try to convince him to purchase a new laboratory instrument.

> **Joe:** *Hi, Mike. Good to see you again.* (wide smile)
>
> **Michael:** (quietly) *Hello.* (no eye contact)
>
> **Joe:** *So how's it going?*
>
> **Michael:** (quietly) *Fine.* (no eye contact)
>
> **Joe:** *Nice day, isn't it?*
>
> **Michael:** *Yes.* (looks down)
>
> **Joe:** *So, what do you think of the new **fantastic** Model 462 Spectrometer? Pretty cool, huh?*
>
> **Michael:** *It is ok.*
>
> **Joe:** *I'd say it's pretty **phenomenal**. Did you notice the high sensitivity level and **spectacular** resolution? And how about the **incredible** wavelength scanning speed?*
>
> **Michael:** (No response. Turns away and starts reading data from a computer.)
>
> **Joe:** *So, Mike. What do you say? You must admit that the 462 is quite **astounding**.*
>
> **Michael:** (non-responsive) *I don't think so.*

Joe: *You must be kidding.*

Michael: *Why should I kid you?* (still reading)

Joe: *I can't imagine how you aren't amazed by the* **unbelievable** *performance of the 462.*

Michael: *How do I know you tell me the truth?*

Joe: *C'mon, Mike. Why would I lie to you?*

Michael: *Because you are a salesman.*

Sales personnel have always needed to understand their potential buyers. In today's marketplace, such knowledge is even more critical. What we observe in this scenario is Michael, a scientist who emigrated from Russia in the 1980s. As someone who went through his formative years in the Soviet Union, Michael learned that the government used the media to advance the role of socialism. Russian citizens understood that little of what appeared in the press could be believed. In fact, there was an old joke that Russian people told about their two newspapers: Isvestia (Truth) and Tass (News). Supposedly, Russians surmised there was no Isvestia in Tass and no Tass in Isvestia.

Joe's attempt to use such superlative adjectives as fantastic, astounding, and incredible to demonstrate the superiority of his product probably appears insincere to Michael. Perhaps these words, which remind Michael of the propaganda he heard in the Soviet Union, are lost on the receiver of the message. If Joe wants to improve his chances of selling to Michael, he should do the following:

- Take time to form a relationship with Michael.

- Uncover the information Michael wants to know about the product.

- Provide information and data, if necessary, from independent sources.

- Employ testimonials from current satisfied customers.

- Never exaggerate the product—always under-promise and over-deliver.

BLOWN AWAY

Chad Miller is a young, energetic boat salesman. He has been working for Sea Cruz for five years and has been successful with the small fishing craft, but has had little success selling the larger luxury yachts. Stan Grabowski and his wife, Judy, are interested in the Sea Cruz 36'. Stan is planning on retiring and would like a boat for relaxing and cruising.

Chad: *Hi folks. I'm Chad Miller. Thanks for coming by.*

Stan: *I'm Stan and this is my wife, Judy.*

Chad: *So, what can I do for you guys today?*

Stan: *We're interested in the Sea Cruz 36'.*

Chad: *Sweet, man. That's one hell of a boat. I mean it's really "rad." Like talk about a rocker!*

Judy: *Rocker?*

Chad: *Whoa! I'll say. That baby has a stereo that will blow your socks off. It even has a built-in ice maker to keep the "Bud" good and frosty. You'll have everyone in the marina partying on your boat.*

Stan: *Well, we're really interested in a boat that we can live on and cruise from time-to-time.*

Judy: *Right. We want a boat that is comfortable for sleeping and good for entertaining our friends.*

Stan: *And don't forget the grandchildren.*

Chad: *Whoa, man! You're blowin' me away. You mean you got grandkids? No way. You can't be old enough.*

Judy: *Thanks, but we have four and one on the way.*

Chad: *Whoa…unreal! Like they are goin' to freak out when they see the Sea Cruz. Man, turn on some tunes and those kids'll be rockin'.*

Judy: *What about the sleeping accommodations?*

Chad: *There's a king-size bed down below, a cuddy bunk, and a convertible table bunk in the salon. Enough room for you two, your kids, and grandkids to crash in. I mean that king-size bed down below might even increase the grandkid population. Down below is what we like to call the "Screw Room" in nautical terms, that is.* (laughs)

Stan: (Not laughing) *Well, Chad, I'm afraid that the Sea Cruz 36' is a little too "rad" for us. We were just looking for some nice peace and quiet, but it seems like this boat is going be a magnet for everyone and their friends and relatives.*

Judy: *Right, Stan. All we need is to have uninvited guests dropping in to "party." Sorry, Chad, but you and the Sea Cruz definitely blew us away.*

The senior market, which controls approximately 50 percent of the wealth in the U.S., is growing by leaps and bounds. One source claims that 10 baby boomers reach the age of 50 every minute. In this scenario, Chad employs a sales pitch that might be appropriate for someone his own age, but the communication turns into disaster when he talks to Stan and Judy. Chad also hurts his message by employing slang and making an inappropriate sexual comment. If Stan and Judy want a boat on which to live and entertain their family, this is what Chad needs to focus on with his sales presentation.

Much of what Chad says is inappropriate for senior buyers like Stan and Judy. In most cultures of the world, older citizens are treated with great respect. Senior citizens from cultures outside the U.S. are offended easily when a salesperson who is from a different age or social group speaks to them as equals and makes disrespectful comments. In this case, Chad speaks out of familiarity of his own culture zone and raises issues that are embarrassing to citizens from most cultures of the world.

Chad may not be the appropriate salesperson to sell a large-ticket, high-involvement item like a Sea Cruz 36'. He has been successful selling smaller boats, perhaps to buyers who are closer to his own age. The dealership has made a mistake by allowing Chad to interact with more mature customers who want to make a major investment in a Sea Cruz 36'. Likewise, senior buyers may not appreciate a young salesperson calling them by their first names. When dealing with senior buyers, it is best to begin by calling them Mister or Misses Jones. If they say, "Please call me Stan," then do so. It is better to show respect than to act too familiar.

For Chad to succeed, which seems highly unlikely in this situation, he must demonstrate mature behavior in all his actions. This includes mature speech and dress, as well as an ability to relate comfortably with older buyers. Given what we have seen with Chad, this may be a difficult role for him to pull off. One strategy the dealer might consider is for Chad to deal with buyers in his own age range and to have a more mature and professional salesperson for larger, more expensive purchases.

THE FRENCH DISCONNECTION

Marie Deveraux grew up in Paris and was transferred by her company to manage the U.S. distribution and marketing of a major French tire brand. She has lived in Montreal and speaks English with only a slight accent. Today, Marie has an appointment with Ron Heath, a TV advertising sales executive.

Ron: *Hello, Ms. Deveraux. It's a pleasure to meet you. Thank you for meeting with me today.*

Marie: *Hello, Mr. Heath. It's nice to meet you.*

Ron: *I will try to be brief, but I have a very attractive offer for you on a prime-time spot.*

Marie: *That means it's probably expensive.*

Ron: *It's a special deal that will give you top coverage in the major U.S. markets. It is especially aimed at the high-end car buyer, and it will air during those controversial news shows.*

Marie: *Controversial?*

Ron: *Yes, you know the ones that dig into political issues like boycotting countries that don't support United States policy?*

Marie: *Ah, you mean like France and Germany?*

Ron: *Well, I know that your tires are French made, but we wouldn't mention that in your commercial. Why remind folks where they're made?*

Marie: *Yes, but we are not ashamed of it. We are very proud that our tires are made in France.*

Ron: *Yes, but it's not something to brag about in this country. I'd say that most Americans would avoid buying French products after all that fuss over U.S. policy.*

> **Marie:** *Then why would I want a spot in the middle of a*
> *show that is centered on raising political conflict?*
> *Au revoir, Mr. Heath.*

One must wonder why Ron would suggest to Marie that she advertise her firm's French tires on a "controversial" television show. Certainly one purpose of television advertising is to reach large numbers of a target market, but the viewers should not be "anti-" a specific country. Perhaps more importantly, what is apparent in this vignette is that Ron has not considered Marie's nationality. As a citizen of France and having lived in Montreal, Marie is proud of her French heritage. To suggest that the advertisement not communicate to viewers the tires' origin is unthinkable, and certainly unacceptable, to Marie.

Unless Ron modifies his approach, Marie will not agree to purchase. Perhaps Ron has an open prime-time spot that he is under pressure to fill. Even so, he must ask himself if this is what is best for Marie's firm. Also, Ron should not raise the political issue of France not supporting the U.S. in the United Nations. This is something that Marie has no role in, regardless of her own personal views. If Ron were monitoring his actions, he would understand that Marie is not receiving his approach positively. He can increase the chances of selling Marie advertising if the slot fits her needs—which may include proudly stating that the tires originate in France.

Had Ron known about Marie's cultural origins in France and Montreal and the nationalistic pride of the French culture, it is unlikely he would have committed these cultural blunders. A salesperson should always steer clear of politics, religion, and other potentially sensitive subjects. As a salesperson in today's marketplace, it is Ron's responsibility to be so informed.

IT'S GREEK TO JACK

Yanis Christofinis was born in Greece and established a family business in the U.S. selling kitchen supplies to restaurants. He and his 22-year-old son, George, have been steadily building the business and are quite proud of their hard work and success. Jack Billings is a salesman for the Freeze Rite Company, a large manufacturer of refrigerators and freezers.

Billings: *Hi, Yanni. How are you doing?*

Christofinis: *Not bad. Not bad.*

Billings: *Looks like you've been doing really well by the looks of things.*

Christofinis: *Yeah. George has been working hard, and we are growing.*

Billings: *And that's why I want to talk with you. We've got some new freezers that'll knock your socks off.*

Christofinis: *I'd like to keep my socks on, thank you.* (smiling)

Billings: *I mean with the new freezer line, you can relax and let Georgie handle most of the business.*

Christofinis: *Yeah. Well I'm not quite ready to retire. I built this business from nothing and took it through the hard times.*

Billings: *Of course, Yanni. I'm just trying to say that it's time to slow down. You know, take some time off. Take a vacation. Maybe go back to Greece. I'm sure the business won't fold if you took some time off.*

Christofinis: *That's easier said than done, Jack. This business is too competitive to take time off.*

Billings: *All I can say, Yanni, is that with the new line of freezers, you won't have to worry much about competition any more.*

Christofinis: *Jack, can I tell you something? You get nothing for doing nothing. This business takes work, hard work, and I've never seen any business succeed that takes the competition for granted. I owe it to George and my family to see to it that we stay on course. I have to worry about the competition. It's simply my duty.*

Billings: *So, does that mean you're not interested in the new line?*

Christofinis: *No. It means that I'm not sure that you fully understand how I do business.*

In the U.S., some citizens dream about making a significant amount of money fast and then retiring to enjoy what they perceive to be a life of total freedom. In other cultures, people view the world quite differently. In this case, Yanis Christofinis does not appear to be looking to retire and let his son take over the business. Yanis is proud of his accomplishments. He came to the U.S. and, through hard work and ingenuity, has become an economic success. He may view the company as an extension of himself and will only hand over the business to his son when he feels the time is correct.

Why has Billings approached the customer with "buy my line of products and you will get wealthy and retire"? Perhaps Billings himself would like to sell his line of products and retire. The salesperson has made several major mistakes. First, such a sales strategy should not be brokered unless it is known for certain that the customer is looking to make money to retire or live the good life. Second, the salesperson must understand the customer. In this case, Billings raises issues that Yanis feels are personal. In many cultures, it is beyond the realm of acceptability for a salesperson to broach money or personal intentions with the customer. Billings has done both.

Yanis sees himself as the patriarch of the family. He has come to the U.S., become a success, and established an avenue for his children to lead successful lives. However, his personal values suggest that he must remain on the job daily to ensure that the business continues to prosper. His values also suggest that he will decide *if* he should hand the reins of control to his son, George. The salesperson may want to take a sales approach that demonstrates the superiority of the product, in comparison to competitors, and how adopting the new line will make the business stronger. In this scenario, Yanis wants to win and Billings should help him succeed.

YOUR PRODUCT IS FINE. WHAT ABOUT THE EXTRAS?

Harry Morgan is an office manager for a large insurance company. He is responsible for purchasing and leasing personal computers and copy machines. Sandra Peterson sells and leases copy machines for Copy Max, a local distributor. This is Sandra's first visit with Mr. Morgan, who has yet to conduct business with Copy Max.

> **Sandra:** *Hi, Mr. Morgan. I'm Sandra from Copy Max.*
>
> **Morgan:** *Yes, come in. Tell me what you are selling. I have very little time.*
>
> **Sandra:** *I would like to introduce you to Copy Max and our—*

Morgan: *Yes, yes, I'm sure you have a good company. It's what you're paid to say. Just tell me why I should do business with you.*

Sandra: *Well, first of all, we are a local distributor so you get personal service.*

Morgan: *But that is what I already get from OptiBuz; I'm good friends with Bob Stanger.*

Sandra: *I know Bob and he's a nice guy, but I think that we can offer superior service.*

Morgan: *Yes, I'm sure you think so. So what can you do that Bob can't do?*

Sandra: *Like I said, we can provide—*

Morgan: *Bob takes good care of me.*

Sandra: *I will take good care of you, too.*

Morgan: *Oh really!!! Do you like to play golf?*

Sandra: *I haven't—*

Morgan: *Bob and I play regularly at his country club.*

Sandra: *Well, that is nice of him, but how does he help you with your copy needs?*

Morgan: *Like I said, Bob takes good care of me. Last week he took me to dinner at the l'Auberge du Cite. It's the most expensive restaurant in town.*

Sandra: *Does that mean I have to do that to earn your business?*

Morgan: *What does your company do for special custom-ers? Maybe a nice trip to Hawaii might get my attention.*

Sandra: *I could talk with my boss about that. So, are you interested in getting the best copy machines with the* *best service available?*

Morgan: *Of course, but it's the little extras that interest me, too.*

Sandra: *Thank you for your time, Mr. Morgan.*

In today's marketplace, women occupy significant selling and buying roles. The majority of college graduates have been female for some time, and this trend will likely continue into the foreseeable future. While most business interactions are professional, there are times when sales calls cross the line of acceptability. This is one such case.

First, there is no situation in which such a request is acceptable. Morgan appears to believe he is in a superior position that allows him to make demands upon the salesperson. For example, note that the current salesperson—who is a male—provides expensive dinners and golf to Mr. Morgan. Perhaps Morgan perceives that salespersons are inferior and must treat him with respect (bribes). While it is not clear from the scenario, Morgan may not place high credibility in female sales reps. Such sexist attitudes are declining in the U.S. but, as mentioned in Chapter 3, they still exist in Japan and most Middle Eastern cultures.

Sandra finds herself in a difficult situation. If she reports Morgan to his superiors, he may be fired, but there is little assurance that her company will receive sales. She could report this to her sales manager, who may then switch the account to a male salesperson. However, Morgan will probably try to auction his services to the highest bidder. The best course of action is to monitor the situation and wait for the next buyer to come on board. Unless Morgan is a relative of the owner, he will eventually be discovered and sacked. Sandra must not give in to his demands and must maintain her professionalism, even though Morgan appears to be unethical.

Female salespersons may face discrimination, but the best way to reduce such behavior is to gain trust, demonstrate superior product knowledge, and keep one's word when promising samples, information, or shipments. Most buyers are more interested in who can provide the highest value for the price and prefer to partner with someone who will work hard to help them succeed.

FREE PRODUCT, BUT PAY FOR THE TRAINING...

Larry Johnson is calling upon Dr. Hershel Bernstein, who moved to the U.S. from Russia. Johnson has only recently been transferred to a large, urban area after selling primarily to buyers in a rural area of the deep South.

Johnson: *Nice t' meetcha, Dr. Bernstein. Howya doin t'day?*

Bernstein: (Russian accent) *Fine. How are you?*

Johnson: *Just "hunky dorry." It's a great day for buying thingamajigs.*

Bernstein: *Vaht have you got?*

Johnson: *For you, buddy, have I got a deal.*

Bernstein: *You mean a discount?*

Johnson: *Better yet. I'm gonna give you our latest model for nothing. Nada. Free. Zilch.*

Bernstein: *So vaht is the hitch?*

Johnson: *No hitch. All we ask is that you attend our training class.*

Bernstein: *Good. Sign me up.*

Johnson: *Great. I'll get you inta our next class. Since you won't be paying for the equipment, we will ask for an enrollment fee for the training class.*

Bernstein: (uneasy) *How much?*

Johnson: *The price of the class will be equal to the price of the new model. Pretty good, huh?*

Bernstein: *Is dees a joke?*

Johnson: *Of course it is. If you don't pay for the equipment, you pay for the training. If you buy the equipment, you get the training for free. I gotchya' on that one, buddy!!!*

Bernstein: *Please leave!!!!!*

This sales encounter, which was witnessed by one of the authors, illustrates how stereotyping and inappropriate humor resulted in the salesman not only insulting the customer, but also inflaming him. In this case, the salesman was accustomed to selling to "good ole boys" in a southern U.S. territory. In the pursuit of the sale with customers from the same sub-culture, the salesperson employed barbed humor and cajoled customers to form relationships. In this case, the buyer was a 55-year-old Russian Jew who had defected to the United States from the Soviet Union in the late 1970s. Dr. Bernstein had experienced ethnic strife as a young man and was not amused by harmless ethnic joking. Such attitudes are common among people who flee their native country because of ethnic harassment or, even worse, persecution. The lesson to be learned from this scenario is that humor should only be employed when it is certain that all parties understand and are not offended by such behavior.

TOO CLOSE FOR COMFORT

Luis Gonsalves was born in Sao Paulo, Brazil, and owns a new chain of fast food restaurants in the Miami area. Bridgette Greenstein speaks a little Spanish and sells newspaper advertising and is hoping to get a sizable contract for a long-term ad campaign.

Bridgette: *"Buenas dias," Mr. Gonsales. It's nice to meet you. "Gracias" for seeing me today.*

Luis: *Ah, yes, Bridgette* (big smile and warm hand embrace). *It's Gonsalves.*

Bridgette: *Pardon me?*

Luis: *My name. It's Gonsal-ves with a V.*

Bridgette: *Oh. Sorry about that.*

Luis: *No problem* (big smile, touches Bridgette's arm). *But, please call me Lou.*

Bridgette: *Okay, Lou* (nervous smile). *So, I hear that your restaurants are becoming quite popular around here.*

Luis: *Oh yes, Bridgette. We are getting very busy* (wide smile, touches Bridgette's hand). *We are even thinking about expanding into other states.*

Bridgette: (Moves hand back slightly) *I see. So, you must be interested in more media exposure.*

Luis: (Moves closer to Bridgette) *Yes, of course. We are already on TV and radio. Have you seen our commercials?*

Bridgette: *Yes* (moving back). *I have seen and heard the commercials for Rio Expresso. Very entertaining. What about newspaper advertising?*

Luis: *Of course, Bridgette. We have advertised in several of the local papers. Seems like we get better results from TV and local radio. You know, the younger crowd.*

Bridgette: *But newspaper coverage can be effective with the kids' parents.*

Luis: (smiling, touches Bridgette's arm) *Yes, but we need to pay a big ad firm lots of money to design the ad.*

Bridgette: (moving away nervously) *Well, that is true, but we can help you save "mucho dinero" by using our own ad staff. They are particularly good working with Hispanic-owned businesses. In fact, many of our staff members speak Spanish fluently.*

Luis: *That is very important here in Miami, but what about Portuguese?* **Obrigado** *for your time today.* **Tchau.**

It is obvious that Bridgette made several missteps in this scenario. First, Bridgette assumed that Luis Gonsalves was Hispanic when, in fact, he was born in Sao Paulo, Brazil. Second, in typical Latino behavior, Luis, or "Lou," quickly ventured into Bridgette's comfort zone. That is, Lou stood extremely close to Bridgette and touched her on the arm as a form of positive non-verbal communication. Salespeople from many cultures become uncomfortable when someone invades their comfort zone. This includes such behavior as standing close, touching, or looking directly into their eyes. As seen in this scenario, Bridgette reacted by moving away from Lou, which only caused him to follow her.

Bridgette would be more effective if she realized that speaking a few phrases of Spanish could be problematic, especially when she was unsure of the recipient's language. However, when one works in a geographical area where another language dominates, the salesperson may want to learn that language. For example, a salesperson in south Florida may want to take Spanish language classes and/or hire a tutor to improve their ability to communicate in the buyer's language.

Being from Brazil does not initially appear to be important in this encounter for Lou. So, Bridgette should discuss her offer in English. However, when she tries to reassure Lou that her staff speaks fluent Spanish, it turns off the potential buyer. Bridgette cannot assume her customer is a Spanish-American simply because he lives in Miami and has a Latino sounding name. In today's marketplace, one can have a Spanish sounding name, but be from such countries as Portugal, Italy, or the U.S. It is the salesperson's job to uncover this type of information during the preparation stage of the sales process, or during the sense-making portion of the introduction stage.

Also important is Bridgette's need to understand Latino culture and to realize that close proximity improves communications. When Lou stands close to her and touches her on the arm, this does not mean he is acting unprofessionally. In fact, this is a positive sign of communication and she must operate within Lou's zone of comfort. Basically, Bridgette must understand the rules of non-verbal communication and then "walk the walk" when meeting with her customers.

TURN OFF THE LIGHTS

Thabit Fauod owns an import company in New Jersey. Fauod is from Egypt, and he imports Egyptian goods into the United States. John Lake, a salesman for BriteTyme Lamp Company, is making a cold call and finds Thabit sitting at his desk in his office.

John: *Hi, I'm John Lake from over at BriteTyme Lamp Company. How are you today?*

Thabit: *Good. I—*

John: *That's great! I was told that you're the person to see about our amazing True Light fluorescent lighting system.*

Thabit: *I'm afraid—*

John: *That's great! Seeing is believing, and once you see our amazing True Light fluorescent lighting system, you won't believe your eyes.*

Thabit: *I don't —*

John: *Great! Let me pop one of our amazing True Light fluorescent bulbs into one of your fixtures and you'll be totally amazed.*

Thabit: *Ah—*

John: *Great, I can get to the one just over your desk. I'll just hop up on your desk and switch the bulbs.* (takes off shoes and climbs up on desk)

Thabit: *But—*

John: *Great!* (switches bulb) *Wow, isn't that amazing? You're getting 62 percent more light than you had before. All I need is your shipping address, and I'll sign you up for a box of 50 bulbs.*

Thabit: *I'm not—*

John: *Great! I'm gonna give you our special introductory package of 25 bulbs for half the price.*

Thabit: *That's not—*

John: *Great! I just need your shipping address.*

Thabit: *I don't—*

John: *Cummon. How do you pronounce your name?*

Thabit: *Thah-beet.*

John: *Okay, Thah-bet. What do you say to such an amazing offer?*

Thabit: *I can only say that you should—*

John: *I know. Take an order for 25 bulbs.*

Thabit: *No. Please listen to me. You said "seeing is believing;" I've seen enough of you. Now, thank you and please replace the old bulb and take the **amazing** one with you.*

This is a classic situation of a salesperson who was trained by his company to make a canned pitch no matter who the buyer. John has the same line for everyone about his "amazing" fluorescent "system." In this encounter, the customer's space was invaded and quickly overtaken by John's aggressiveness. Constantly interrupted, Thabit was undoubtedly annoyed by John's behavior, yet he patiently waited for the moment when he could dismiss John with grace.

Indeed, John was following the pitch that he'd been trained to use, but had no regard for the customer's needs or feelings. This is unacceptable behavior in any selling situation, but with most Middle Eastern buyers, a relationship must precede the product pitch. It is also taboo to show the bottom of one's shoes to Middle Easterners, let alone taking off one's shoes and standing on the buyer's desk. John also showed a total lack of respect by mispronouncing Thabit's name immediately after hearing it. An excellent practice is to repeat the buyer's name after hearing it until you say it correctly. If you are still uncertain after hearing the buyer pronounce his own name the first time, respectfully ask the buyer to repeat his name slowly.

Also at fault here is the BriteTyme Lamp Company. By training its sales reps to make overly aggressive canned pitches, BriteTyme violates the rules of professional selling and reinforces the old stereotype of the pushy salesperson.

6

SELLING SUCCESSFULLY OUTSIDE YOUR CULTURE ZONE

You have accomplished much. First, you learned how to recognize that culture impacts sales encounters and makes them more complex. You also learned that you must never stereotype buyers from other cultures with whom you meet and form relationships. Next, you explored culture and cross-cultural communications to master the eight areas that complicate and derail interactions between salespersons and buyers. In Chapter 4, a cross-cultural sales process provided a general framework for succeeding in today's marketplace. In Chapter 5, we offered eleven individual scenarios where inappropriate cultural actions led to disaster. At the end of each case, we discussed what happened and explained how a salesperson with a wide culture zone could safely navigate the cultural minefield. Now, let's put all this information into a short and helpful lessons-learned section that is organized around the three-step process of: *recognize, respect,* and *reconcile.*

RECOGNIZE THE ROLE OF CULTURE

To improve your chances of successfully interacting with and selling to buyers from other cultures, you must first understand your own cultural blueprint. Remember the impact of ethnocentrism discussed in Chapter 3. For example, if you were born and raised in the U.S., you tend to be individualistic and egalitarian, have masculine goals, and be less concerned about uncertain situations. It is imperative that you remain aware of how your cultural beliefs influence your perceptions and relationships with buyers from both your own and other cultures.

RESPECT OTHER CULTURES

This means you can never stereotype or oversimplify your perceptions of another person or cultural group. Everyone acts differently, and no two people from the same culture will act exactly the same in every situation. You must start with the *big* picture of cross-cultural interactions to sensitize yourself to potential buyer attitudes and behaviors. Asian-Americans and African-Americans want to interact in a culturally appropriate and sensitive way that results in trust and a lasting connection.[1] This means you should expect to make additional calls and spend greater time forming relationships. When you meet with buyers from cultures that rank lower on the individualistic scale, you should consider the importance of group behavior, but at the same time realize that everyone is an individual who can, and probably will, act differently. The first step in using general information about cultural groups is to find a starting point for planning the best approach to these customers.

RECONCILE CULTURAL DIFFERENCES

Listed below, in Table 6-1, are general cultural scores for a number of important economic nations whose citizens conduct business both in the U.S. and globally. Additionally, most recent

TABLE 6-1:
Cultural Dimension Ratings for Selected Cultures

Country	Power Distance	Individualism	Masculinity	Uncertainty Avoidance
U.S.	40	91	62	46
Great Britain	35	89	66	35
Germany	35	67	66	65
Australia	36	90	61	51
Japan	54	46	95	92
Spain	57	51	42	86
Taiwan	58	17	45	69
South Korea	60	18	39	85
France	68	71	43	86
India	77	48	56	40
Arab Countries	80	38	53	68
Mexico	81	30	69	82
Philippines	94	32	64	44

*Adapted from Gert Hofstede, *Cultures and Organizations*, London: McGraw-Hill Book Company, 1991.

citizens of the U.S. have emigrated from the nations on the list.

Given the general information about citizens from specific cultures, we list sales interaction recommendations in Table 6-2 that are based upon the cultural norms shown above. Remember that the higher the scores the greater the likelihood that members of this culture adhere to *power distance* (acceptance of unequal social strata), *individualism/collectivism* (viewing a situation based upon how it impacts the individual or group), *masculinity/femininity* (goals of wealth, success, power vs. quality of life,

TABLE 6-2:

Sales Approaches Based Upon Cultural Dimensions

Dimension	Low	High
Uncertainty Avoidance	Share info with many Less need for examples Start with bottom line Challenge status quo	Learn and follow rules Provide success examples Provide cost analysis Share needed information Follow formal channels Comply with procedures
Power Distance	Use influencing skills Plan a give-and-take discussion Encourage questions	Use senior sales reps Use formal presentation Anticipate questions
Individualism	Consider group goals Stress group benefits Longer decision time	Explain benefits to buyer

Masculinity	Stress quality of life/
	   people
	More sensitive
	   negotiation
		Stress money and
		   materiality
		Expect tougher
		   negotiation

nurturing members of a culture), and *uncertainty avoidance* (minimizing surprises in social interactions).

Now, let us combine Tables 6-1 and 6-2 to plan a sales strategy for a buyer who was born in Taiwan but now lives in the U.S. An *uncertainty avoidance* rating of 69 is higher than that for the U.S. (46), so a formal approach is recommended. That is, learn how business is conducted, discuss successful customers, provide cost analysis and needed information, and follow formal purchasing rules prescribed by the buyer. *Individualism* is very low (17), so remember that group goals will predominate and you should expect decisions to take longer. Try to weave the benefits to the group into your sales communications. *Power distance* (58) is higher than the U.S., so it is important to show respect and use job titles, unless otherwise instructed. Lastly, and perhaps most importantly, remember these are beginning points that may have to be adjusted based upon the individual buyer's personality. Additional information about selected cultural influences for nations is provided in Appendix 3.

WORK, WORK, WORK AT CROSS-CULTURAL COMMUNICATION

As a salesperson, it is your job to communicate effectively with potential buyers. This means you need to recognize that there is more than one way to communicate, and it may differ from your current approach. Also remember to utilize correct voice tone and volume, body language, and demeanor. If a breakdown in communication should occur, look for ways to get back on track rather than faulting yourself or the buyer. Effective cross-cultural communications include:

- Never stereotyping, but thinking about the individual buyer
- Speaking slowly and clearly—not louder!
- Being direct and specific with your language
- Emphasizing key words
- Allowing the buyer to read your lips
- Organizing your thoughts

- Allowing time for the buyer to listen and understand

- Asking open-ended questions to gauge buyer understanding

- Being polite and steering clear of inappropriate humor

- Offering the buyer a "win-win" business proposition

Also, laying the foundation for meetings, through careful planning, is extremely important. As discussed in Chapter 3, the pre-approach step of the sales process allows the salesperson an opportunity to anticipate potential cross-cultural problems and prepare for the sales encounter. Thus, the salesperson can anticipate potential *faux pas* and be as prepared as possible for each meeting.

An important point to remember is that you must construct your sentences carefully so that you communicate as clearly as possible. When you plan what you are going to say, the likelihood of making careless *communication mistakes* is greatly minimized. Although this sounds like a simple suggestion, actually pulling it off is more difficult. Another recommendation for speaking English with greater clarity includes steering clear of idioms, slang, double-meaning words, and jargon. Remember, *idioms* are words that have no translatable meaning: "a firm estimate" or "a working vacation." *Slang* refers to words or phrases such as "What's up?" or "We're having a summer blowout!" *Double-meaning words* include: running (exercising or a motor that is operating), steaming (mad or in a manufacturing process), and fire (to terminate or heat). *Jargon* refers to words that are invented to describe new technology. A current example is "microbots," which describes miniature robots that travel through the body looking for actual and potential medical problems. Other examples of jargon include: telemarketing, undercover marketing, and relationship marketing. The problem is that in our cross-cultural interactions with buyers, such terms are employed frequently and unconsciously. To clearly communicate with our cross-cultural customer, the usage of such language must be minimized.

LISTEN ACTIVELY AND EMPATHETICALLY

A salesperson is *empathetic* when they put themselves in the mindset of someone else. Some sellers tend to talk most of the time; however, buyers prefer salespersons who listen and understand their needs and concerns. One expert recommends making your presentation to Asian customers and then remaining quiet, rather than continuing to talk.[2] Thus, in cross-cultural selling, it is doubly important to listen, look for non-verbal communications, and try to sense what the buyer is feeling. In cross-cultural sales interactions, such behavior will likely keep you near the edge of your current culture zone.

HONOR BUYER CHOICES

You must honor the decisions made by the cross-cultural buyer, whether they buy your product or not. If the buyer decides to purchase from you, congratulations! You must have offered a great product to the buyer in such a way that you met both their business and cultural expectations. If the decision is "no, thank you," then you should suspend judgment and examine the situation as an outsider. Did you correctly interpret the buyer's needs? Did you approach the buyer correctly? Did you utilize effective cross-cultural communications? Were your interactions culturally sensitive? Was your offer a "win-win" situation?

Did you respond promptly and effectively to buyer questions and concerns?

Hopefully, if you did not win the contract or make the sale, the buyer will explain why he or she made that decision. However, you should understand that buyers, especially those from other cultures, are normally reluctant to discuss your firm's shortcomings. In many cultures, people are unwilling to be candid in order to maintain group tranquility and avoid conflict or "save face." This means it is quite possible that you will never learn what you could have done to "get the business." This is why it is so important to use your perceptiveness to monitor meetings and evaluate the quality of all communications and discussions.

LEARN (AND PROFIT) FROM EACH ENCOUNTER

It is likely that you will make mistakes when selling to cross-cultural customers. You should not dwell on your mistakes or say, "If only I had done…" It is more productive to tell yourself, "Next time I'll…" Salespersons who are perceptive, monitor their performance, recognize potential problems, and work hard to correct unintentional mistakes will be more successful in cross-cultural settings. In fact, salespersons who make many small errors and correct them learn faster. Said differently, if a salesperson defines "error" as the bottom 35 percent of performance, he or she will continue to improve. Conversely, if a salesperson only considers the bottom 5 percent of performance to be an error, it will be easier to overlook them. Learning from error correction is very important in cross-cultural sales encounters.[3]

WHAT DOES THE FUTURE HOLD?

There is little doubt that the need to sell cross-culturally will accelerate in the future. More firms are entering the global marketplace, which means they are selling in more nations and hiring buyers and technical persons from many diverse countries. Likewise, the number of women completing college and moving up the corporate ladder will increase. In the U.S. and Europe, professionals from different cultures continue to take positions of responsibility in large corporations and small businesses. These trends suggest that the role of the salesperson must include the skills necessary to successfully interact with buyers from distinct cultures, ethnicities, religions, and genders. Without cross-cultural skills, salespersons will be at a disadvantage when meeting with potential buyers. This book provides you with a framework and tools for selling more effectively with buyers from another culture, gender, religion, or ethnicity.

RESOURCES

A number of references can be consulted to learn more about the specific cultures of customers. This is the last time we are going to say this: remember that a country's general cultural norms are important, but individual buyers do not always follow exact norms. That is, all members of a culture do not act or behave in a standardized fashion. This is because human behavior is shaped by a combination of cultural, background, family, education, and individual personality variables. The resources listed in Appendix 4 offer general guidance for planning initial meetings and identifying areas the salesperson should approach with caution.

HOW YOU CAN HELP

As you engage in cross-cultural selling, you will learn from your unintentional mistakes. If you would like to share an anecdote with the authors, please forward your experiences to: ehoneycutt@elon.edu or GRAtrainer@ec.rr.com. Insightful examples of cross-cultural selling successes and mistakes will be incorporated into the next edition of this book. No company or person will be identified in any illustration submitted, and we will obtain written permission to use your specific example in the next edition of *Selling Outside Your Culture Zone*. Now, go forth and succeed!

APPENDIX 1

WHAT'S YOUR CULTURE ZONE QUOTIENT (CZQ)?

Before reading this book, you might want to know where you stand regarding awareness and sensitivity to the cultures of your potential customers. The goal of this book is to demonstrate to sales personnel the advantages to be gained by understanding the buying habits of consumers from other cultures. Hopefully, this increased understanding will lead to greater empathy and an enthusiastic appreciation for your customers' heritage. But first, what is your current CZQ?

Take the test below to gain a starting point score. After reading *Selling Outside Your Culture Zone*, take the test again. We know your score will significantly improve. It follows then, that as your CZQ score increases, so will your sales figures when you interact with buyers from other cultures.

Select the one correct answer for each question:

1. Minority group members now make up ____ percent of U.S. households and account for ____ percent of annual consumer spending.

   a. 10, 10   b. 10, 20

   c. 20, 20   d. 25, 20

   e. 50, 50

2. What percentage of U.S. residents were born in another country?

    a. 2%   b. 5%

    c. 12%   d. 20%

    e. 25%

3. If Kimche is on the menu, you are probably in a(n) _____ restaurant.

    a. Japanese   b. Cambodian

    c. Korean   d. Indonesian

    e. Hungarian

4. This airline would not serve you an alcoholic beverage.

    a. Thai Air   b. Aeroflot

    c. Air India   d. Pakistan Airlines

    e. Olympia Airlines

5. According to the U.S. Census Bureau, the number of non-Caucasian residents in the United States will _____ by the year 2050.

    a. Increase   b. Increase significantly

    c. Remain the same d. Decrease

    e. Decrease significantly

6. Your customer's native language is Farsi. He is from:

    a. Saudi Arabia   b. Farsinia

    c. Sri Lanka   d. Yemen

    e. Iran

7. Your customer has a mezuzah on the right side of his office doorway. This person's religion is:

    a. Jewish   b. Hindu

    c. Shinto   d. Mormon

    e. Shiite

8. Which of the following cities is also a country?

    a. Amsterdam   b. Colombo

    c. Singapore   d. Mexico City

    e. Santiago

9. Which of the nations listed below is now known as Kampuchea?

    a. Bombay   b. Belgium Congo

    c. Persia   d. Cambodia

    e. Leningrad

10. Your customer grew up in the former Soviet Union. He is from:

    a. Ukraine   b. Bulgaria

    c. Czech Republic   d. East Germany

    e. Afghanistan

11. When communicating with a buyer from another culture, an idiom may cause confusion. What is an idiom?

    a. Words that have multiple meanings.

    b. Careless words.

    c. Words that have no literal translation.

    d. Inappropriate humor.

    e. Using a synonym for idiot.

12. What gift would be inappropriate for a Hindu customer?

    a. A bottle of scotch whiskey

    b. A brightly colored necktie

    c. A gift certificate to a Chinese restaurant

    d. An after shave cologne

    e. A leather wallet

13. It would be unwise to give a set of four golf balls to a(n)
    _____ customer.

    a. Chinese   b. Italian

    c. Austrian   d. British

    e. Pakistani

14. Dancing with handkerchiefs and shouts of opah are heard at
    _____weddings.

    a. German   b. Japanese

    c. Jewish   d. Greek

    e. Zulu

15. Your customer is absent from work during two or three days
    in the autumn. She is probably _____.

    a. Muslim   b. Jewish

    c. Buddhist   d. Deist

    e. Jehovah's Witness

16. What is the official language of Quebec?

    a. English   b. Spanish

    c. Haitian   d. Dutch

    e. French

17. How does your Brazilian-born customer thank you in his native language?

    a. Obrigado   b. Gracias
    c. Grazie   d. Arigato
    e. Danke

18. Which one of the following countries was Taiwan part of prior to 1949?

    a. Vietnam   b. Thailand
    c. China   d. Philippines
    e. Britain

19. How much wealth does the Baby Boom generation control?

    a. 30%   b. 40%
    c. 50%   d. 55%
    e. 60%

20. When communicating with buyers from other cultures, you should not:

    a. Speak loudly so the customer will hear you.
    b. Be direct and specific with your language.
    c. Allow time for the buyer to listen.
    d. Steer away from inappropriate humor.
    e. Think of the customer as a person rather than stereotyping.

Turn to page 111 to review the correct answers and learn how you did.

Answer the following questions by selecting a number between 1 and 5. If you "strongly disagree" with the statement, circle 1. If you "strongly agree" with the statement, circle 5.

1	2	3	4	5
Strongly Disagree			**Strongly Agree**	

1. I have many friends that represent different races, origins, or linguistic backgrounds.

    1   2   3   4   5

2. I regularly eat diverse ethnic foods.

    1   2   3   4   5

3. I listen more closely to people with accents.

    1   2   3   4   5

4. I enjoy learning about diverse customs and cultures.

    1   2   3   4   5

5. I treat people equally well, no matter what their ethnic background.

    1   2   3   4   5

6. I enjoy visiting non-English speaking countries.

    1   2   3   4   5

7. When visiting other countries, I try to learn some of the local language.

   1   2   3   4   5

8. I enjoy selling to a diverse customer base.

   1   2   3   4   5

9. I am very patient with customers from other cultures.

   1   2   3   4   5

10. I know the names of political leaders of Canada, Mexico, and Great Britain.

   1   2   3   4   5

Go to page 114 for an explanation of how your total score compares with salespeople with wide culture zones.

APPENDIX 2

ANSWERS TO WHAT'S YOUR CULTURE ZONE QUOTIENT (CZQ)? QUIZ

1. D   Minority members residing in the U.S. now comprise 25 percent of households and account for 20 percent of annual consumer spending.

2. C   Twelve (12) percent of U.S. residents were born in another country.

3. C   *Kimche* is often called the national dish of Korea.

4. D   Pakistan Airlines, being the national airline of a Moslem nation, would not serve alcoholic beverages on their flights.

5. B   According to the U.S. Census Bureau, the number of non-Caucasian residents in the United States will increase significantly by the year 2050.

6. E   *Farsi* is the national language of Iran and differs from Arabic.

7. A   A *mezuzah* is a piece of parchment inscribed on one side with texts from Dueteronomy in 22 lines and on the other side with the name of God, rolled and put into a case, and attached to the doorpost of the house as commanded in the Biblical passage.

8. **C**   Singapore is a 400 square mile city-state located at the hub of Southeast Asia. Singapore is one of the most modern and economically prosperous areas in the world.

9. **D**   Cambodia, located between Vietnam and Thailand in Southeast Asia, is now officially named Kampuchea.

10. **A**   Ukraine was a Soviet Socialist Republic and the other countries listed were "allies" of the former Soviet Union (Russia).

11. **C**   *Idioms* are words that have no literal meaning—for instance, to tell a customer that the product being sold has all the "bells and whistles." While this means the product has all the appropriate accessories and capabilities, it literally has no meaning unless one is aware of the phrase.

12. **E**   Hindus generally revere cows and would be offended by the gift of a leather wallet.

13. **A**   In Japan, China, and Korea, the word for the number four sounds like the same word for "death" or "to die." Therefore, four is considered to be the unluckiest number.

14. **D**   Greek.

15. **B**   There are two Jewish Holidays in *Tishri* (approximately October): *Rosh Hashana* and *Yom Kippur*.

16. **E**   The official language of Quebec is French, stemming from colonial days.

17. **A**   "Thank you" in Brazilian Portuguese is *Obrigado*.

18. C Taiwan became the Republic of China in 1949 when Mao Tse-tung's People's Republic of China government seized power in Beijing. The governments of China and Taiwan have remained hostile toward one another for more than 50 years.

19. C The Baby Boomer generation, born between 1946 and 1964, controls 50 percent of the wealth in the United States.

20. A When communicating with buyers from other cultures, you should *never* speak loudly in hope of increasing your communication effectiveness.

NOW SCORE YOURSELF:

16 or more correct You have a wide culture zone and should be successful in many cross-cultural sales situations.

12–15 Your culture zone is average, so you may miss a few sales opportunities.

9–11 You have a somewhat narrower culture zone, so you may be losing some key sales.

5–8 Your culture zone is somewhat minimal, so you could be missing out on quite a few sales opportunities.

Less than 5 Your culture zone is minimal, so you could be missing out on a lot of sales opportunities.

Statements 1–10 allow you to rate your culture zone by behavior. Total the number you circled for each statement, and based upon your total score, look at the scale below:

42–50   Suggests you have a wide culture zone

35–41   Suggests you possess an average culture zone

25–34   Suggests you exhibit a narrow culture zone

Below 25   Suggests you have a minimal culture zone

APPENDIX 3

DOING BUSINESS
WITH INDIVIDUALS FROM...

Arab Community

Remember that not all Middle Easterners are Arabic.

Be courteous and harmonious in all communications.

A buyer's dignity, honor, and reputation are important.

Close personal relationships are desired.

Sitting or standing back is considered rude.

Handshakes are preferred, but not too firm.

It is more important to get acquainted rather than to be concerned with time.

Nothing happens quickly, so be patient.

Wait for your hosts to raise business topics.

When negotiating, both parties should be of similar status.

Never point with your finger or show the soles of your feet.

If you are left-handed, apologize before signing a document.

Never give alcoholic gifts.

It is considered too personal to ask about a buyer's spouse or female children.

Australia

Australians are outgoing, relaxed, and have a sense of humor.

Non-verbal gestures are used to clarify speech.

Speech is generally direct and frank—pretensions are disliked.

Close friendships are valued highly.

Dress can be informal, but business dress is formal.

Work is seen as a means to live, not "living to work."

Use of the "OK" hand sign or "V" for victory may be perceived as rude or vulgar.

Yawning in public is considered rude.

Sportsman-like gestures are appreciated since good sportsmanship is highly respected.

It is appropriate to give your business card, but you may not receive one in return.

Australians may be more formal at the beginning of a meeting, so wait for them to move to less formal communications.

China

China is a collectivist, or group-oriented, society and the interests of many parties must be considered in all business interactions.

It is important to arrive on time. Bilingual business cards are essential.

Trust and mutual connections (guan-xi) are to be emphasized.

Meetings may begin with pleasantries until business begins.

Chinese are tough negotiators but stick to their word.

Long-range benefits are important.

"Slow down" tactics may be used on sellers who are perceived to be impatient.

Chinese politics should not be discussed.

Proper etiquette is important: dignity, patience, sensitivity, and respect.

Numerous sales calls should be expected to consummate the business deal.

France

French citizens are friendly and humorous, but they can be sarcastic.

Personal honor and integrity are valued. Salespersons should not boast.

Personal questions are to be avoided until a relationship is established.

French conversation is not linear, and frequent interruptions should be expected.

In French firms, decisions are made by senior executives.

Quality of life (feminine perspective) is important.

Neatness in dress and good taste are important.

Germany

Germans tend to be linear thinkers, so detailed planning is valued.

Time should be organized for the greatest efficiency.

Be punctual and well-prepared for all meetings.

The preferred time for business meetings is late morning and late afternoon.

Salespersons should be conservative and subdued.

Third-party introductions are best.

Always use titles, such as "doctor," or "professor," when
appropriate.

One's private life should only be discussed among close
friends.

Do not brag about personal achievements and finances.

Sit with the soles of your shoe facing away from a German
buyer.

Great Britain

Maintain appropriate behavior and avoid casualness; loud
noises are taboo.

Initially focus on business and do not ask personal questions.

Respect and distance are extended to those superior or
affluent.

In negotiations, seek to understand the other side's position.

Tolerance, compromise, and problem solving are stressed.

Listen carefully to ensure you understand distinctly British
terms.

Appropriate manners and behavior are expected at all
social occasions.

Business should be avoided when socializing.

India

Avoid using first names, unless asked to do so by the buyer.

Always use titles, such as "doctor" or "professor."

Always show respect to Indian women.

Family and friends are important influences in Indian
decisions.

The left hand may be considered unclean by Moslem or Hindu Indians; therefore, use the right hand to give or receive items. Apologize if you must sign with your left hand.

Personal questions should be avoided. Expect to bargain for goods and services.

Many Indians believe that a higher power controls their destiny.

Italy

Many Italians are creative problem solvers who seek solutions via family and friends.

Relationships are extremely important to Italians.

Appearance, behavior, and preparation are all important in business negotiations.

Image is important; proposals and presentations must look good.

Be punctual in meetings, act conservatively, and follow the lead of the buyer.

Italians are basically fatalistic—little can be done to change destiny.

Buyers may be reluctant to state specific objectives due to their belief in destiny.

Italians may multitask or take calls during business meetings.

Sellers are expected to be on time but also show flexibility.

Italian culture is high context—words are vague and the listener must fill in the meaning.

Status and titles are important—thus, Italians are high in power distance.

Italian companies are risk averse and prefer pragmatic business decisions.

Japan

Group or collectivist aspirations and achievements are stressed.

Third-party introductions are important. Always use bilingual business cards.

Order, propriety, and appropriate behavior are expected between superiors and subordinates.

Japanese are polite and disciplined but may behave differently to strangers.

When confronted with the unexpected and strange, the Japanese may laugh inappropriately.

An atmosphere of energy and cheer is preferred.

Wait patiently for meetings to move beyond formality.

Logical approach to communication is insufficient—emotion, as to a friend, is essential.

Japanese outlook tends to be cautious, and stalling tactics are often employed.

Decisions generally take longer and are made after achieving group consensus.

Mexico

It is important to demonstrate respect in all meetings.

Differences attributed to status, age, or gender are often maximized in conversations.

Status consciousness is related to family, wealth, school, position, and authority.

Communications tend to be high context—one must listen carefully and try to understand both what is said and what is meant.

It is imperative to learn the buying process and to know the buyer well.

Wait before talking business.

Personal connections are important.

Mexicans expect the seller to practice courtesy, dignity, tact, and diplomacy.

Social competence is critical—vigorous handshakes are signs of respect.

Mexicans sit and stand close together, so expect to work in close proximity.

Be on time for appointments, but do not be surprised if you have to wait.

Trust is based on both the buyer's intuition of the seller and the seller's performance.

Mexicans tend to be risk-averse in their purchase decisions.

Philippines

Conflict is to be avoided at all cost. Silence or evasive speech will preserve peace.

A Filipino may say "yes" to mean: yes I hear you, yes I understand, or yes I agree.

The business card should be presented at the end of the first meeting.

Filipinos are generally warm and friendly.

It is essential to look for non-verbal communication signals.

When negotiating, make sure every detail is discussed to reduce uncertainty.

Business relationships take time to cultivate.

Personal relationships are more important than a written contract.

Filipinos are loyal friends and expect reciprocal loyalty.

Always show respect for elders and the Philippine family.

Russia

Russians may expect high-level executives to visit to confirm their importance.

Russians may initially act uninterested, but this will soften in private and over time.

Business dress should be conservative.

It is common to ask for multiple bids and then to play one seller off against another.

In negotiations, discuss all business aspects before quoting a price. Otherwise, expect negotiations to be reopened after the price quote to include training or other essentials.

Do not believe that granting concessions now will lead to future business.

Written rather than oral agreements will be honored.

Always adhere to protocol or a standard process when negotiating.

South Korea

It is presumptuous and impolite to address a Korean by his name. It is better to say "Good Morning," without adding the surname.

In every relationship, individuals are viewed in a hierarchy—higher or lower.

Saying "no" can insult. "Yes" may be said even though it is not meant.

Praise is important to keep business relations on an even plane.

At meetings, everyone is treated with great care; use humor cautiously.

Do not initiate business conversations on important issues. Begin with minor issues and move to new business or delicate matters at the end of the sales call.

Changes in the economy, politics, or personal conditions can invalidate a contract.

Koreans move with deliberation, dignity, and caution in business dealings.

Korea is a high-context culture; always look for non-verbal nuances.

Always show respect for elders.

Spain

Spaniards enjoy their life, so time is viewed more leisurely.

Salespersons should be punctual in their appointments.

Bilingual business cards are essential, with the Spanish side up for presentation.

Establishing business relationships takes time and may be linked to eating/socializing.

Business discussions can be lively and laborious.

Business dress should be formal.

Project a positive image through your actions and attire.

First names are generally not used in business meetings unless initiated by the buyer.

United States

Individual aspirations and achievements are encouraged.

U.S. businesspersons tend to be friendly and open in their actions.

Americans tend to focus on the tangible aspects of the job.

Americans are low-context communicators—words over non-verbal gestures.

Persuasion is most often based upon logic and analytical arguments.

Buyers prioritize to control the allotted time.

Americans trust the information presented is correct unless shown differently in earlier negotiations.

Americans are generally risk-takers.

Individual buyer decisions are made that must then be cleared with superiors.

Contractual agreements are used to formalize negotiations even after a handshake.

APPENDIX 4

ADDITIONAL RESOURCES

Suggested resources for learning more about cross-cultural communications, interactions, and behavior.

Business Across Cultures, Fons Trompenaars and Peter Woolliams, Chichester, England: Capstone Publishing Ltd., 2003.

Riding the Waves of Culture, Fons Trompenaars and Charles Hampden-Turner, New York: McGraw-Hill, 1998.

Sales Management: a Global Perspective, Earl D. Honeycutt, Jr., John B. Ford, and Antonis Simintiras, London: Routledge Publishers, 2003.

An Introduction to Intercultural Communication, Fred E. Jandt, Thousand Oaks, CA: Sage Publications, Inc.

Do's and Taboos of Humor Around the World: Stories and Tips from Business and Life, Roger E. Axtell, New York: John Wiley & Sons, Inc., 1999.

Managing Cultural Differences, Philip R. Harris, Robert T. Moran, and Sarah V. Moran, Amsterdam: Elsevier Butterworth Heineman, 2004.

Multicultural Manners: New Rules of Etiquette for a Changing Society, Norine Dresser, New York: John Wiley & Sons, Inc., 1996.

Do's and Taboos Around the World for Women in Business, Roger E. Axtell, Tami Briggs, and Margaret Corcoran, New York: John Wiley & Sons, Inc., 1997.

Dun and Bradstreet's Guide to Doing Business Around the World, Terri Morrison, Wayne A. Conaway, and Joseph J. Douress, Englewood Cliffs, NJ: Prentice Hall, 2000.

Gestures: The Do's and Taboos of Body Language Around the World, Roger E. Axtell, New York: John Wiley & Sons, Inc., 1998.

Kiss, Bow, or Shake Hands: How to do Business in Sixty Countries, Terri Morrison, Wayne A. Conaway, and George A. Borden, Avon, MA: Adams Media Corporation, 1995.

Bridging Cultural Barriers for Corporate Success, Sondra Thiederman, Lexington, MA: Lexington Books, 1990.

REFERENCES

Preface:

1. "Hispanization: Three new ideas" (2005), The Goldman Sachs Group, Inc., October 7.

2. Vence, Deborah L. (2005), "Asian media grows, firms take note," *Marketing News,* June 1, 11.

3. Westphal, David (2005), "Hispanics drive population growth, *The News & Observer,* Raleigh, NC, June 9, 3A.

4. Thiederman, Sondra (1991), *Bridging Cultural Barriers for Corporate Success,* Lexington, MA: Lexington Books.

5. Selling Ethnicity Inc. (2004), Time Archive, September 20, http://faculty.smu.edu/oseaney/files/1302 /immigration/research.

6. Jandt, Fred E. (2004), *An Introduction to Intercultural Communication,* Thousand Oaks, CA: Sage Publications, Inc.

Chapter 1:

1. Hoppe, Michael H. (2004), "Introduction: Geert Hofstede's Culture's Consequences: International Differences in Work-Related Values," *Academy of Management Executive,* 18:1, 73–74.

2. Trompenaars, Fons and Charles Hampden-Turner (1998), *Riding the Waves of Culture,* New York: McGraw-Hill, 6.

3. Thiederman, Sondra (1991), *Bridging Cultural Barriers for Corporate Success,* Lexington, MA: Lexington Books.

4.   Trompenaars, Fons and Peter Woolliams (2003), *Business Across Cultures*, Chichester, England: Capstone Publishing Ltd.

Chapter 2:

1.   Chang, Julia (2003), "Multicultural Selling," *Sales & Marketing Management*, October, 26.

2.   Weise, Elizabeth (2005), "French mechanics and English cooks may be just fine, study finds," *USA Today*, Friday, October 7, 9A.

3.   Harris, Philip R., Robert T. Moran, and Sarah V. Moran (2004), *Managing Cultural Differences*, 6th Edition, Amsterdam: Elsevier, Butterworth, Heinemann.

Chapter 3:

1.   DuPraw, Marcelle E. and Marya Axner (1997), "Working on Common Cross-Cultural Challenges," Topsfield Foundation.

2.   Reynolds, Nina and Antonis Simintiras (2000), "Toward an Understanding of the Role of Cross-Cultural Equivalence in International Personal Selling," *Journal of Marketing Management*, 16, 829-851.

3.   Hofstede, Geert (1991), *Cultures and Organizations*, London: McGraw-Hill Book Company.

4.   Hodge, Sheida (1998), "Feng Shui: A Realtors' Guide for Increased Sales to Asians," Professional Training Worldwide.

5.   Wong, Angi Ma (1993), *Target: The U.S. Asian Market*, Palos Verdes, CA: Pacific Heritage Books.

6.   Chang, Julia (2003), "Multicultural Selling," *Sales & Marketing Management*, October, 26.

7.   Lewis, R.D. (1996), *When Cultures Collide: Managing Successfully Across Cultures*, Nicholas Brealey Publishing Limited.

8. Jandt, Fred E. (2004), *An Introduction to Intercultural Communication*, Thousand Oaks, CA: Sage.

9. Thiederman, Sondra (1991), *Bridging Cultural Barriers for Corporate Success*, Lexington, MA: Lexington Books.

10. Roces, Alfredo & Grace (1998), *Culture Shock: Philippines*, Portland, OR: Graphic Art Center Publishing Company.

Chapter 4:

1. Hoffman, Jennifer (1998), "Selling Across Cultures," *Tierra Grande*, Publication 1260.

2. Honeycutt, Earl D., John B. Ford, and Antonis C. Simintiras (2003), *Sales Management: A Global Perspective*, London: Routledge.

Chapter 6:

1. Suarez-Hammond, Sonya (2005), "Respect cultural values to connect with buyers," *Marketing News*, September 1, 30, 36.

2. Wong, Angi Ma (1993), *Target: The U.S. Asian Market*, Palos Verdes, CA: Pacific Heritage Books.

3. Trompenaars, Frons and Charles Hampden-Turner (1997), *Riding the Waves of Culture*, New York: McGraw-Hill.

INDEX

ABOUT THE AUTHORS

*The authors bring more than 55 years of practical
and academic expertise to the formulation of this book.*

LEW KURTZMAN, President of Growth Resource Associates, has more than 30 years of experience in direct sales, international marketing, and sales training in over 30 countries on five continents. Much of Lew's experience includes training in global and cross-cultural situations.

EARL HONEYCUTT is Professor of Business Administration (Marketing) at Elon University, N.C. After serving as a U.S. Air Force B-52 flight officer in the Strategic Air Command (SAC) and completing an M.B.A., Earl worked in industrial sales for an electronics division of TRW, Inc. and then earned a Ph.D. in marketing, with extensive sales training research, at the University of Georgia. For more than two decades Dr. Honeycutt has focused his research on sales and B2B issues both in the U.S. and in other cultures. He has published more than 175 articles on sales topics and B2B marketing and co-authored two textbooks: *Business-to-Business Marketing* (2001) and *Sales Management: A Global Perspective* (2003). Dr. Honeycutt also serves as the Associate Editor of *Industrial Marketing Management* and on the Editorial Review Boards of the *Journal of Personal Selling & Sales Management, Journal of Business-to-Business Marketing,* and *Journal of Selling & Major Account Management.* He has taught classes in Japan and the Philippines, served as the Air Force Reserve specialist on the Philippines, and traveled to more than 40 nations around the world.